The Sacred and the Profane:

An Investigation of Hipsters

Jake Kinzey

Winchester, UK
Washington, USA

First published by Zero Books, 2012
Zero Books is an imprint of John Hunt Publishing Ltd., Laurel House, Station Approach,
Alresford, Hants, SO24 9JH, UK
office1@o-books.net
www.o-books.com

For distributor details and how to order please visit the 'Ordering' section on our website.

Text copyright: Jake Kinzey 2010

ISBN: 978 1 78099 034 7

A CIP catalogue record for this book is available from the British Library.

Design: Stuart Davies

Printed in the UK by CPI Antony Rowe
Printed in the USA by Offset Paperback Mfrs, Inc

We operate a distinctive and ethical publishing philosophy in all
areas of our business, from our global network of authors to
production and worldwide distribution.

The Sacred and the Profane:

An Investigation of Hipsters

CONTENTS

Dedicated to Aunt Jane, Ken Winterbottom,
William Roberts PhD and Liz Pis.

"Don't pull me down, this is where I belong
I think I'm different, but I'm the same and I'm wrong
Don't pull me down, this is where I belong
I think I'm different, this is where I belong"
Blink 182 – "Pathetic"

Chapter One

The hipster has been understood in many ways, but most popular explanations are false, misleading, or at best a small piece of a larger picture. An example is N+1 Magazine's recently published *What Was The Hipster?* The title suggests that the hipster is no longer with us (R.I.P.), but this couldn't be further from the truth. The hipster is neither dead nor buried. The children of the hippies and yuppies live! in the streets, the malls, the media, the cities and the suburbs the world over. Ironic postmodern-kitsch zombies are finding comfort in the apathy and over-consumption of late-capitalism. Is there anything new to say about the hipster? Hasn't the subject already been endlessly analyzed in books, magazines, newspapers, and blogs, etc.? Who cares? Isn't it "just another" subculture?

Another way to understand the hipster is through Apple's well-known 1984 Superbowl Ad. Apple introduced their new line of personal computers to the general public in a well-known parody (or is it pastiche?) of 1984.[1] The commercial is set in a grey dystopic industrial setting, with shots of a Big Brother-like figure talking to people who all look the same. Then there are full-color shots of a nameless heroine, a track star carrying a hammer, representing Apple. She throws the hammer into the screen and destroys it, "liberating" the grey populace.

This commercial can be read in many ways: the shift from "centralized" capitalism to "decentered" capitalism; the shift from TV to the computer; but the most powerful message the commercial seems to send is "are you bored and confined within your grey late capitalist world? Do you feel like a lifeless automaton? Buying an Apple computer will revolutionize you and bring creativity and color to your life!" Today it's easy to see how these late-capitalist hopes are utopian (in the negative sense). Rather than endless creativity we are still stuck in conformity. An easy test is going into any college lecture hall of reasonable size and looking up: one is bound to see a sea of illuminated Apples staring back at them. The white Apple headphones became so ubiquitous that they made people easy targets for thieves on the New York subway. It seems like we have gone back to *1984*; yet people seem to believe in bringing "creativity" and "authenticity" to their lives more than ever. By now it has become a truism that being anti-mainstream *is* the mainstream: here one is able to locate the truth in the typical assertion that hipsters "think they are being different but really act the same."

But, while this is undoubtedly true, that is not enough to properly explain what is going on. *Why* do they all act the same, and *why* is the appearance of being unique *necessary* to the process? The platitude doesn't acknowledge what is distinctive about the hipster, while being able, at the same time, to show similarities to other subcultures. What is a hipster? The hipster has clearly identifiable progenitors (the bohemians, the beats, the (post-) punks etc.) but is not explained away in a narrative of previous subcultures. When asked, most people describe the hipster in terms of concrete objects they consume (what they wear, listen to, eat etc.) or as an attitude (e.g. they are elitist snobs masked in an "aesthetic populism"). They make the same mistake as critics who examine the hipster in isolation rather than seeing their place in larger processes (i.e. global ones). Hipsters are *the* most postmodern "mainstream-subculture" to date and are perfectly integrated into postmodern late-capitalism (à la Frederic Jameson).

Since there has been no "dominant" mainstream culture for a while, hipsters have reluctantly filled this empty place with their own question mark. Hipsters rarely refer to themselves as "hipsters," seeing themselves as beyond labels. If hipsters do acknowledge that something like a hipster exists, they will be glad to show you that hipsters exist "out there," having nothing to do with themselves. *Distance* and *irony* are key concepts in understanding this outlook. Hipsters rarely passionately believe in anything, preferring cynical distancing.

The hipster was born in the era of globalization driven by free-market fanaticism; they represent the socio-economic realities around them. It is no surprise to hear that, "Across the developed world, from Copenhagen to Cape Town, from Tokyo to Sao Paolo, from Kreuzberg [in Berlin] to Williamsburg [in New York]– from Grangemouth to Guildford, for that matter – today's [hipsters] all wear the same clothes and accessories, listen to the same sounds, ride the same bicycles, and read the same magazines, e-mailouts and style blogs."[2] What started as a small movement in New York can now be found on giant billboards worldwide; the hipster is the dominant aesthetic filter through which mainstream culture emanates.

The hipsters' quest for perpetual cool is sustained by endless cultural imperialism: everything is potentially for the taking. In typical postmodern fashion, it seems as if nothing they do is really *new*, it's all about sampling, bricolage, remixing, or, usually, just stealing wholesale from the past. They decontextualize and take fashions and ideas from cultures that they have little knowledge of to make their lives into a "work of art." This need for *uniqueness* and pure authenticity usually has the peculiar effect of making their "aesthetic lives" into something like a postcard of Andy Warhol's *Campbell Soup Cans*: a copy of a copy, mass-produced and unoriginal. In their attempt to achieve absolute individuality, hipsters somehow overlook the fact that they are doing the exact same thing in the same exact ways as everyone around them.

Mark Greif asked whether the "1999 model of the hipster" is the true hipster like "the way those from the late 1950s and early 1960s who fit the Maynard G. Krebs caricature were the only actual beatniks [i.e. the pre-Hippies], and the San Francisco arrivistes in 1967 were the only true hippies [...] or is hipster a kind of permanent cultural middleman in hypermediated late capitalism, selling out alternative sources of social power developed by outsider groups, [a bunch of] infiltrators who spoil the resistance—the coolhunting collaborators and spies"?[3] One of the aims of this work is to show that hipsters are, in a way, infiltrators and spies. Not only that, but there has never been an "authentic" or "original" hipster. What gets lost in this notion is that *selling out is practically programmed into the hipster.*

The rise of the hipster has, of course, stimulated "anti-hipster" sentiment; as the Boston Globe comments, "mocking hipsters has become a national sport." Like Jameson's observation on postmodernism, hipsters have permeated so much of the social sphere that is hard to say how much of it has affected us (have you looked in your closet lately to see how much it's changed over the past few years?); the hipster, like postmodernism is all around us. This why laughing at the various follies of hipsters can be entertaining, but taking a purely negative (or positive) stance on the hipster is unhelpful and unproductive. To get what the hipster is all about, one must think *through* the thick fog of present thought. In light of this, this text tries to really understand the hipster, and thus must go beyond mere value judgments.

Notes

1　Most people believe this book is a warning against totalitarianism and communism/socialism in particular, almost never learning that Orwell was a socialist. Thus, *1984* should be read as a warning against the excesses inherent within *both* Stalinism (state-socialism in general) *and* capitalism.

2　"Meet the global scenester: He's hip. He's cool. He's everywhere." *The Independent*, August 14, 2008, http://www.independent.co.uk/life-style/fashion/features/meet-the-global-scenester-hes-hip-hes-cool-hes-everywhere-894199.html

3   Rob Horning, "The Death of the Hipster." *Marginal Utility*,
    http://www.popmatters.com/pm/post/the-death-of-the-
    hipster-panel/

Chapter Two

Nero: The Proto-Hipster? (An Early Case Of The "Original-Unoriginal")

In-between running the Roman Empire and attempting to seduce his mother Aggripina, was Nero the proto-hipster? There are many others who would fit the description, but Nero is quite unusual in that he presided over the largest empire then known to mankind. The image of a powerful Roman emperor on a fixed-gear bike in thrift store clothes is paradoxical (and anachronistic), but there is truth in the image if one replaces fixed-gear biking with chariot racing.

Just as hipsters enjoy dabbling in pop culture, Nero[1] scandalously (at least for the elites of his day) embraced what were considered to be commoner's interests. "Nero had long desired to drive in four-horse chariot races. Another equally deplorable ambition was to sing to the lyre, like a professional [...] There was no stopping him."[2] Those around Nero tried to appease him by building a private track "where he could drive his horses, remote from the public eye." But, as Tacitus accounts in horror, "soon the public were admitted – and even invited; and they approved vociferously. For such is a crowd: avid for entertainment, and delighted if the emperor shares their tastes."

Nero aspired to be a poet as well, but his work lacked "vigor" and "inspiration,"[3] like hipster (I hesitate to use the word) "art." Tacitus implies that these shortcomings were due to his method of composition: "[Nero] gathered round himself at dinner men who possessed some versifying ability but were not yet known [...] they strung together verses they had brought with them, or extemporized – and filled out Nero's own suggestions, such as they were."[4]

Hipsters, some claim, blur traditional gender differences. In his own violent way, didn't Nero precede them?: "Having tried

7

to turn the boy Sporus into a girl by castration, [Nero] went through a wedding ceremony with him – dowry, bridal veil and all – which the whole court attended, then brought him home and treated him as a wife."[5] On a different wedding night he "imitated the screams and moans of a girl being deflowered."[6]

These similarities alone wouldn't qualify Nero as a proto-hipster, but his slumming, perhaps the essential component of the hipster aesthetic and lifestyle, seals it. A general definition of slumming would be consuming Otherness (culturally/economically/sexually etc.) but always from the distance and position of social advantage. A good example is in Guy de Maupassant's *Bel-Ami*, the story of the rise of Georges Duroy (nickname Bel-Ami) through late 19th-century Parisian society. Duroy and his girlfriend Clotilde "would go into working-class cafes, sitting down at the back of the smoky hovel, on rickety chairs, at an old wooden table"[7] with Clotilde "repeating: 'I just adore this. I like slumming. I find this more fun than the Café Anglais [i.e. an middle/upper class establishment].'"[8] Usually those slumming try to fit in and pass along relatively unnoticed but end up sticking out. This is due not only to their ingrained social habits, but also to their (conscious or unconscious) desire to show that they are still above what they are participating in.

> Clotilde would wear a coarse cotton dress, her head covered by a bonnet like that worn by the lady's maid in a farce, and, despite the elegant and studied simplicity of her outfit, she would still be wearing her diamond rings, bracelets, and earrings, explaining, when [Duroy] begged her to remove them: "Nonsense, they'll think they're rhinestones." She believed herself wonderfully disguised.[9]

Her "camouflage" was easy for the regulars to see through and "the waiter would stare in astonishment at this strange couple, as he placed before them two glasses of brandied cherries."[10] The narrator describes Clotilde drinking the brandied cherry, drawing attention to how the experience for her is trangressive:

> trembling, frightened, and enthralled, she would begin sipping the fruity red juice, gazing round her with uneasy, excited eyes. Every cherry she swallowed gave her the feeling of committing a sin, every drop of the burning, spicy liquid going down her throat gave her a fierce pleasure, the pleasure of a wicked, forbidden gratification.

Also, those slumming usually seek thrills by fantasizing about an element of possible danger (whether real or imagined):

> ...[Clotilde] walked out quietly with her head bent, the way an actress walks off stage, passing between the drinkers who, leaning their elbows on tables, watched her with a suspicious, annoyed air; and when she was through the door she would give a great sigh, as if she had just escaped from some terrible danger.

Nero, too, loved slumming but he was exponentially more mischievous than Bel-Ami and Clotilde. He was the Emperor and had practically unlimited access to all kinds of entertainment; and yet, "dressed as a slave," Nero loved to "make a round of the taverns or prowl the streets [of Rome] in search of mischief."[11] Some of his favorite activities included stealing items from stores and beating up travelers. Nero would "break into shops, afterwards opening a miniature market in his home with the stolen goods, dividing them up into lots, auctioning them himself, and squandering the proceeds." Most hipsters would be content with going out to a party, bar, show, club, gallery opening, etc, and calling it a night; Nero enjoyed "attack[ing] men on their way home from dinner, stab[bing] them if they offered resistance, and then drop[ping] their bodies down the sewers." If many of those slumming have only imagined fears, Nero "often risked being blinded or killed – once he was beaten almost to death by a senator whose wife he had molested, which taught him never to out after dark unless an escort of military tribunes was following him at a discreet distance."[12]

Hipsters merely live and play in "established" slums/blighted areas, Nero had the bright idea to build his own "red-light" district: "Whenever [Nero] floated down the Tiber to Osita or crusied past Baiae, he had a row of temporary brothels erected along the shore, where a number of noblewomen, pretending to madams, stood waiting to solicit his business."[13] "In the wood which Augustus had planted round his Naval Lake, places of assignation and taverns were built, and every stimulus to vice was displayed for sale."[14] Not intending to "shut down the mall" like today's stars do, Nero saw that "there were distributions of money. Respectable people were compelled to spend it; disreputable people did so gladly."

Though Nero was far more violent, wealthy and powerful than your average bohemian, the two are closer together (conceptually) than they may appear at first glance. Today, commentators emphasize "boheminization" and its spread throughout mainstream culture, particularly within the "white-collar" middle/upper classes. Finding the link between today's "bohemia-writ-large" and proto-hipster/bohemians like Nero requires investigation into the 19th century origins of modern bohemia, which lead to the hipster we know.

From Bohemian Paris to "Poser" Globalized: The Genealogy of the Hipster

Bohemia
Why are "financially successful people flatter[ing] themselves by dressing up as bohemians" while "a working-class store like

Sears seeks to boost itself not by offering up images of a well-appointed family home, but by changing its slogan to 'The Good Life,' as though it were some exclusive realm of luxury"[15]? The answer's origins are in modern bohemia, which began in 19th century Paris, on the heels of the French Revolution, the establishment of industrial capitalism in England, and their by-product, modernity. The bohemians, together with the dandies, are the first subcultural antecedent to the hipster. Like the hipster, the bohemian is unthinkable without the background of capitalism; the difference being that the hipster emerging under a much more pervasive and total capitalism than did bohemia.

Much of what we know as the "modern" world can be traced back to the English industrial revolution and the French Revolution. Eric Hobsbawm claims in *The Age of Revolution* that "the revolution which broke out between 1789 and 1848 [...] forms the greatest transformation in human history since [...] men invented agriculture and metallurgy, writing, the city and the state. The revolution has transformed, and continues to transform, the entire world."[16] The revolutions in France and England would eventually spread all across the world.

> The great revolution of 1789-1848 was not the triumph of 'industry' as such, but of *capitalist* industry; not of liberty and equality in general, but of *middle class* or *'bourgeois' liberal* society; not of the 'modern economy' or 'the modern state,' but of the economies and states in a particular geographical region of the world (part of Europe and a few patches of North America), whose centre was the neighbouring and rival states of Great Britain and France.

Paralleling capitalism's growth, bohemia eventually extended across the world. The world before this period was *overwhelmingly* rural (90% or more in most countries). Industrialization brought droves from the countryside into cities, which became ideal conditions for the growth of bohemia. Bohemians differed from the Romantics (the group often thought to have preceded the Bohemians) in that they embraced urbanity. Since then, the idea of bohemia has always been inseparable from the city.

Liberal-capitalism's expansion had major effects on the art world. Artists before had mostly relied on "aristocratic, state, or institutional patronage,"[17] but the decline of the noble classes and rise of the bourgeois weakened the traditional patronage system. Artists now had to sell their goods in the marketplace: "the commodification and commercialization of a market for cultural products during the nineteenth century [...] forced culture into a market form of competition that was bound to reinforce processes of 'creative destruction' within the aesthetic field itself."[18] The artist was "cut off from a recognizable function, patron or public and left to cast his soul as a commodity upon a blind market, to be bought or not; or to work within a system of patronage"[19] which was in general "economically untenable." It cannot be overemphasized how important this shift was within the field of culture. Art was now "an individual effort forged under competitive circumstances"[20] that led to "each and every artist [seeking] to change the bases of aesthetic judgement, if only to sell his or her product." Therefore, it became necessary, if one wanted to eat, "to produce a *work of art* [...] a cultural object that would be original, unique, and hence eminently marketable at a monopoly price." The artist "had to assume an aura of creativity, of dedication to art for art's sake," which gave off the impression that the artist was naturally creative and self-generating. The result was a focus on the individual and an obscuring of the artists' relation to his predecessors, peers or society at large. Artists increasingly became portrayed as "mad geniuses," or those "who stood alone, shouting into the night, uncertain even of an echo."[21] Therefore, "it was only natural that [the artist] should turn himself into the genius, who created only what was within him, regardless of the world and in defiance of a public whose only right was to accept him on his own terms or not at all."

The idea of the "mad genius" comes from the Romantics, as well as the associations of "artistic eccentricity" with looser sexual morals, "a casual attitude towards conventional manners and hygiene, and a propensity to nurture extravagant moods with drugs and alcohol."[22] Today this behavior could be called mainstream, but in their day the bohemians were quite scandalous. Linking deviance and the "artistic temperament has become among the most persistent characteristics of bohemia as a style of life."[23]

What linked a relatively diverse group of people (bohemia) together was their disdain for bourgeois values. The bohemians overlapped a lot with the dandies, who could also not stand the bourgeoisie, but the bohemians made poverty a virtue whereas dandies put on aristocratic airs. Dandyism began in England and found its way to France becoming enmeshed with the politics of the French Revolution. The gilded youth, or the beginnings of dandyism in France, was a self-consciously political statement of dressing in an aristocratic style to distinguish themselves from the sans-culottes, or the lower classes.

In addition to the "looser morals" they shared with the dandies, bohemians did not value the accumulation of wealth and had little money. Besides, it is not like many of them had a chance to make a lot of money anyway: 'geniuses' were "in general not only misunderstood but also poor."[24] They cherished the idea of art for arts sake, and living out one's dream even if it meant poverty. It is assumed that most bohemians were artists, but this is untrue; a good proportion of bohemia was composed of people who were just there to hang out and have fun. Bohemia became indentified with *living one's life as if it were a work of art*. This usually meant trying to cultivate *the most unique personality*.

Another myth of bohemia is that it was mostly composed of individuals of considerable talent; instead it was filled with mostly hacks. Bohemia is best seen, as Balzac commented, as "a stimulating interlude until the chance for real work arrives."[21] Bohemia, then is like a lottery: "for most, that chance would never come, and [...] the existence of a numbers game [...] inevitably produce[d] far more losers than winners."[22] Far from being wiped out, this game "is among the most durable features of the artists' experience, continuing through the present day."

The Avant-Garde
In the late-nineteenth century, what would become more widely known as the avant-garde surfaced for the first time. There would always be bohemians, but the avant-garde represented a new era. Fredric Jameson's split between realism/ modernism/postmodernism can help locate these movements within the greater historical picture at the time. His three-part schema is derived from Ernest Mandel's three-part division of stages within capitalism, each a further expansion of capitalism across the globe. "After the political triumph of the middle classes," there is "*national capitalism*, a capitalism of a classical type in which exchange and production take place within the borders of individual advanced countries."[23] This "first stage of national capitalism corresponds [...] in literature and culture to what one may call the moment of realism, dominated by [...] realistic forms and artistic languages and, of course, by the common sense of philosophical conceptions."[24] With Bohemia commencing in the era of national capitalism, it can best grasped as within (both accepting and resisting) the larger movement of *realism*. The avant-gardes arrived "towards the end of the nineteenth century" which saw the creation of the "second stage" i.e. "what has been [...] called by Lenin and others the *monopoly* stage or the stage of *imperialism*." This included "the amalgamation of business into large national monopolies and then the carving up of the world into a set of spheres of influence controlled by classical colonial powers." "The moment of

monopoly capitalism or of *imperialism*" is "the moment in which modernism [...] emerges." So the avant-gardes largely belong to the cultural logic of *modernism*. In fact, "it was only in an era of speculation in future and fictious capital formation [like the kind that gave rise to the 2007 crisis] that the concept of an avant-garde [...] could make any sense."[2]

The avant-garde movement was marked by a sense of urgency. They found themselves "in the real moment of commencement. The nineteenth century announced, dreamed, and promised; the twentieth century declared it would make man, here and now."[26] This, Alain Badiou claims, is "the *passion for the real*," a concept "provid[ing] the key to understanding the century."[27] For the avant-garde, art is not the "production of eternity, the creation of a work to be judged for the future."[28] Instead the avant-gardes wanted "a pure present for art. There [was] no time to wait." Having a pure present for art also connects to a larger avant-garde theme: *erasing the boundaries between everyday life and art*. Among other things, this vision entailed "dismantl[ing] the institutional autonomy of art, eras[ing] the frontiers between culture and political society and return[ing] aesthetic production to its humble, unprivileged place within social practices as a whole."[29]

Also key was the avant-garde's reaction to the economy and culture becoming more integrated (or the further commodification of the cultural sphere). In using *modernist* forms, the avant-gardes created works to "resist commodification" and "[hold] out by the skin of [their] teeth against those social forces which would degrade [them] to [...] exchangeable object[s]."[30] Their works were often difficult, open ended and resistant to easy meaning and passive assimilation, i.e. how the "masses", "bourgeois" (or both) approached works of art. There may have been a general disdain of the masses among the avant-garde (as among bohemians and dandies), but "certain avant-gardes - Dadaists, early surrealists – tried to mobilize their aesthetic capacities to revolutionary ends by fusing art into popular culture."[31]

Either way, a growing "mainstream" culture was virtually impossible for the avant-gardes to ignore, whether they embraced it, rejected it, or sought a third position. It was a product of Fordism, a system of capitalist arrangements appropriate for the age of centralization, giant factories and the Model T. In the United States, where the "foundational myth is that of the frontier and the cowboy individualist, its twentieth century increasingly demanded that workers live in cities [like the avant-garde which was primarily urban] and labor as if practically identical cogs in a machine."[32] Workers in industrialized countries (particularly in factories) were supposed to take on relentlessly repetitive and dull tasks thanks to the advent of Taylorist management. Most avant-gardes lived in cities, but refused to labor as "identical cogs in a machine," recoiling in fear before the image of a Fordist automaton and seeking refuge in a *unique, personal,* or *authentic* style. The particular ways that modernism shaped our understanding of these ideas has been vital in the creation of the modern day hipster.

Beats, Hippies, Punks, Hip-Hop, Hipsters

After World War II, the center of the art world moved from Paris to New York. The bohemians, dandies, and avant-gardes had originated in Europe, while most of the upcoming subcultures had their roots in the United States, which had emerged out of World War II as *the* superpower of the capitalist world. The Beats wanted nothing to do with the 1950s suburbanized hell-hole that America had become after World War II. Amidst McCarthy-Fordist-conformism they let it be known through their writing and lifestyle that they were rejecting the mainstream and seeking "authenticity," which, from the 1950's onwards, became a dominant theme within subculture. The Beats began as a group of writers in New York City.[33] Like the bohemians (and much of the avant-garde), the Beats did not mind the gritty and dirty. They mixed the high and the low, and it's no surprise that Allen Ginsberg heard the voice of god[34] while masturbating. The Beats wrote about drugs, free love, homosexuality, roaming, eastern spirituality, i.e. NOT about barbecues in the backyards of suburban nuclear families and the like.

Also in New York, the Abstract Expressionist painters achieved prominence with their sprawling canvases of abstract color fields, and "were bound by a desire to challenge the notion that art needs be in the service of literature, that art needs to illustrate."[35] Jackson Pollack's "drip paintings" consisted of him gathering his "authentic" energy,[36] standing over a canvas on the floor and throwing, dripping and splattering paint onto it. In another example of the mingling of high and low, amongst other items, cigarette butts and flies have been located under the paint of Pollock's paintings. Also important, in the context of the hipster aesthetic (which is largely derived from the post-war New York underground scene), is that the Abstract Expressionists "helped transform the public's image of the artist from that of a gentleman painter in a well-appointed studio to something almost proletarian." The image of the artist as a bohemian was imprinted within the imagination of the masses (who in 1950s America were rather conservative). However, not all was quiet, even in the mainstream. While Elvis swung his hips, appalling the conservatives, rock and roll was being born in America. It's hard for us to imagine the innocent music we hear today being the music of Satan for many back then. But, it is a good illustration of the explosive force of rock and roll.

In the 1960s, one of the Beats, Neal Cassady, became a part of the Merry Pranksters, a collection of acid-dropping proto-hippies lead by writer Ken Kesey. They in turn, became connected with various groups such as the Hell's Angels and the Grateful Dead. At the same time the British Invasion (i.e. the Beatles, Rolling Stones etc.) was sweeping the United States.

With these moments, among others, the "60s" had begun, a period in which many thought that everything was possible. By the end of the 1960s, so much had changed that the hum drum 1950s seemed ancient history.

In the United States, the post-war "baby boom," G.I. Bill, and rising middle class flooded universities with new students. Most had parents that never went to college. Before the 1950s, going to a place of higher learning was, for the most part, an elite experience. Gathering a generation of people raised in opposition to the elites within places of higher learning was asking for radical change. This, mixed with tons of free time (compared to the rest of society), the twin forces of rock and roll and mind-altering drugs, and general global upheaval gave rise to revolutionary sentiments.[37]

There was a general divide (but with plenty of overlapping) between the New Left and the counterculture (to state the difference a bit bluntly: the politically engaged vs. the "tuned out"). The 1960s counterculture, without a doubt, centered around the hippie, who sought authenticity. While more associated with the urban earlier on in the "60s," as the decade drew to a close, the hippie sought more and more to be one with nature. The hippies took many of their cultural cues from the Beats. Many of the Beats embraced the hippy movement (Allen Ginsberg taking on something of a godfather role); but some - like Jack Kerouac, who was conservative – hated and opposed the hippies. Rock and roll, free love and drugs combined to make the "psychedelic." "Expand your mind!"[38] seemed to be the reigning theme. Another was "Fuck the Man!" To many, this meant getting rid of the old system for a new, better one. If the New Left took that as a cue to do things like rallying against the Vietnam War (alongside other colonial projects), opposing racial segregation (at least in the United States), and fighting to overthrow capitalism, the counterculture showed more interest in eradicating the Protestant ethic (saving and eschewing instant gratification), and going against prevailing mainstream culture.[39] Both shared the idea of embracing the present: for the New Left it was about creating a new world *now* by changing the political-economic system. Meanwhile, the counterculture was content to think about enjoyment for the present moment; saving and waiting were too passé. Many in the counterculture thought changing the "system" by trying to revolutionize the economy or political system was a waste of time; they did not see anything peculiar in thinking that, for instance, taking acid was what was *really* going to bring about change.

The hippies were part of a much larger "counter-cultural and anti-modernist movement [...], antagonistic to the oppressive qualities of scientifically grounded technical-bureaucratic rationality as purveyed through monolithic corporate, state, and other forms of institutionalized power."[40] It was a movement that drew upon the energies of an intense period of worldwide class struggle and was "centered in the universities, art institutes, and on the cultural fringes of big-city life." It "spilled over into the streets to culminate in a vast wave of rebelliousness that crested in Chicago, Paris, Prague, Mexico City, Madrid, Tokyo, and Berlin in the global turbulence of 1968." While the movement accomplished a great deal, especially at the level of everyday life, it was "a failure, at least judged in its own terms." By the mid-1970s it was clear the revolution had been stopped or rolled back in most of the world. This failed movement "has to be viewed [...] as the cultural and political harbinger of the subsequent turn to postmodernism. Somewhere between 1968 and 1972 [...] postmodernism emerge[d] as a full-blown though still incoherent movement." By the 1960s, modernist works had become part of the cultural canon, making them appear (to many) complicit with the "system." It was time for something different.

Postmodernism was a sign that something very significant was occurring: another major shift within capitalism. After

World War II, many changes, such as "decolonization and neoco-lonialism [...] the emergence of great multinational corporations, the spread of business to parts of what had hitherto been thought to be the third world"[41] and the invention of new technologies (particularly in the area of communication), culminated in what is called *late capitalism* (or post-Fordism). In developed countries, predominantly industrial economies were transformed to "post-industrial" economies, based around the service and financial industries. More and more children were required to go to college for these jobs, which were often little more than "blue-collar" white-collar jobs, creating a large segment of "overeducated" people. Also important is what is now called "globalization," which is part of late capitalism. Postmodernism, then, is the name for the cultural shifts that happened alongside the change from imperialist capitalism to late capitalism. "The economic preparation of postmodernism or late capitalism began in the 1950s [...] Culturally, however, the precondition is to be found [...] in the enormous social and psychological transformation of the 1960s, which swept so much of tradition away on the level of *mentalities*."

There is plenty of skepticism within modernism, but "the most startling fact about postmodernism" is "its total acceptance of the ephemerality, fragmentation, discontinuity, and the chaotic [...] It does not try to transcend it, counteract it, or even to define the 'eternal and immutable' elements that lie within it. Postmodernism swims, even wallows, in the fragmentary and the chaotic currents of change as if that is all there is."[42] Meta-narratives[43] were smashed to pieces, if only to make room for new, implicit (and therefore more invisible) meta-narratives. It is not hard to see how reactionary times can produce such thought: the failure of the '68 movement turned many into bitter cynics.

The *co-opting* and *mainstreaming* of the counterculture by the "system" was happening at the same time on an unprecedented scale; watching *Dazed and Confused*[44] proves once again that capitalism "is the most elastic and adaptable mode of production that has appeared thus far in human history."[45] It consumes rebellion and spits out conformity (profits included) like nobody's business. Besides the calls for a more democratic economic system or the shrinking of the worldwide military industrial-complex, liberal-capitalism absorbed most of the revolutionary demands of the 1960s (in its own way of course!) without much trouble. You want to smoke weed? Read *High Times*, buy Eazy Widers, but don't get caught! Free love? No problem, *and,* you can make it more fun with sex toys! Women want equality? Why not, we *could* use some more potentially productive recruits in the workforce.[46] Postmodernism presents a situation where "aesthetic production today has become integrated into commodity production more generally: the frantic economic urgency of producing fresh waves of ever more novel-seeming goods (from clothing to airplanes), at ever greater rates of turnover, now assigns an increasingly essential structural function and position to aesthetic innovation and experimentation."[47] Culture has become more and more central in profit-making. A comparison of the mid-nineteenth-century Parisian art scene with the 1980s New York art scene illustrates thus point nicely: "the two thousand or so artists who practiced in or around Paris in the mid-nineteenth century, with the 150,000 artists in the New York region who claim professional status, exhibiting at some 680 galleries, producing more than 15 million art-works in a decade (compared to 200,000 in late nineteenth-century Paris)."[48] This is just one example of something more extensive, for example in the U.S.:

Through most of the century, proportional rate of growth in this population was steady but unspectacular - until 1970. Thus, from 1900 to 1970, the number of artists, writers, and performers per 100,000 of the population in the United States went from 267 to 385, an increase of 44 percent. By 1999, the proportion had jumped to 900 per 100,000, an increase of 237 percent in just three decades. In absolute terms, the number of artists, writers, and performers grew from 791,000 in 1970 to almost two and a half million in 1999.[49]

Also, "since 1973, money has been 'de-materialized' in the sense that it no longer has a formal or tangible link to precious metals [...] or for that matter to any other tangible commodity." This causes "exchange rates between the different currencies of the world" to be "extremely volatile. Fortunes could be lost or made simply by holding the right currency during the right phases."[50] In this postmodern-late capitalist environment,

> money consequently became useless as a means for storing value for any length of time [...] Alternative means had to be found to store value effectively [...] Buying a Degas or Van Gogh in 1973 would surely outstrip almost any other kind of investment in terms of capital gain.[51]

David Harvey concluded that "it can be argued that the growth of the art [...] and the strong commercialization of cultural production since around 1970 have a lot to do with the search to find alternative means to store value under conditions where the usual money forms were deficient."

Culture was in many ways the means of recuperating declining profits in traditional manufacturing because "tremendous emphasis has been put in recent years on finding ways other than straight production of goods and services to make profits."[52] There has been a

> shift away from the consumption of goods and into the consumption of services – not only personal, business, educational and health services, but also into entertainments, spectacles, happenings, and distractions. The 'lifetime' of such

services (a visit to a museum, going to a rock concert or movie, attending lectures or health clubs) though hard to estimate, is far shorter than that of an automobile or washing machine.[53]

Of course, part of the shift towards consumption of services was the seeking of *authentic* experiences. (Why consume like the "average Joe"?) To speed up turnover time on tangible goods, manufacturers made them more "disposable." Another big change in consumption was

> The mobilization of fashion in mass (as opposed to elite) markets [which] provided a means to accelerate the pace of consumption not only in clothing, ornament and decoration but across a wide swathe of life-styles and recreational activities (leisure and sporting habits, pop music styles, video and children's games and the like).[54]

As the 1970s dragged on it became clear to many that subculture had been institutionalized. Mainstream music had become a bloated carcass in comparison to the swinging 60s (glam and prog rock being examples of this shift). To a newly emerging group later known as the punks, this was a completely unacceptable state of affairs. They were part of the postmodern shift in music, the other two important genres being hip-hop and techno. "The punk subculture [...] emerged to fight [...] the normalization of subculture itself, with [...] new forms of social critique and style."[55] Attaching themselves to the raw and visceral, punk wanted to be a complete negation of everything the system stood for, which now included the hippies: "At the heart of early punk was calculated anger. It was anger at the establishment [...] the allegedly soft rebellion of the hippie counterculture [and] the commodification of rock and roll."[56] Do-it-yourself (D.I.Y.) was key to what punk stood for. Fuck the corporate record labels. Get wasted,[57] rip through three/four cord songs. It sounds like something anyone could do, but that was the point. English punk was started "by working class youths decrying a declining economy and rising unemployment, chiding the hypocrisy of the rich, and refuting the notion of reform."[58] It was born more out of material deprivation than early American punk, which was mainly "a middle-class youth movement, a reaction against the boredom of mainstream culture." Wherever they were located, punks wanted to avoid selling-out like the hippies and other subcultures before them. They "promised to build a scene that could not be taken [over and co-opted]. Its anger, pleasures, and ugliness, were to go beyond what capitalism and bourgeois society could swallow. It would be untouchable, undesirable, unmanageable." In light of the previous history, it should be no surprise that this "promise" proved impossible to keep.

Picture capitalism as a tiger shark, which can "eat almost anything, from turtles to birds, as well as other sharks and fish. Besides normal prey they even eat garbage like tires, nails or car license plates, as sometimes documented by examinations of their stomach contents."[59] Because of this, tiger sharks "acquired the reputation of being 'garbage eaters' and were considered primitive. In reality, it is exactly their diverse food palette and unique chewing mechanism which today puts them into a different light, for their apparent lack of specialization indicates a much higher development. Tiger sharks are special because they feed on a broad spectrum of prey rather than being specialized on specific prey." To capitalism, there is no essential difference between selling Chanel dresses and selling torn-up punk clothes. This indifference has made it quite adaptable. In the end, it had no problem turning punk into a profitable enterprise. Punk was thought by many to have begun in 1975-1976; by 1978 Crass was declaring "Punk Is Dead."

Movements such as hardcore punk and post punk tried to fight the commercialization of punk. Hardcore punk was also reacting to new wave, a movement that arose alongside punk (in fact for some time they were part of the same scene). New wave had a smoother, glossier texture than punk, featured more complex song-writing, did not mind dabbling in the artificial (the use of synths and drum machines being examples), and enjoyed more immediate commercial success. New wave, hardcore punk, and post punk begat "indie,"[60] which includes a lot of different styles, but can be summed up as a post-punk movement combining bohemian and punk aesthetics, holding on tight to the concept of D.I.Y. In the hipster aesthetic, the do-it-yourself idea (whether actually realized or just faked) holds a central place. Holding onto the D.I.Y. idea is supposedly going against the mainstream, but a closer inspection shows it to be all over the mainstream. Billionaire Facebook co-founder Mark Zuckerburg apparently slaughters his own meat, in order to better appreciate the life of the animal that is providing him with food. "Home improvement" stores like Home Depot or Lowe's love to portray themselves as providers of tools and other goods for do-it-yourself home improvement. And when is the last time you got a piece of furniture from Ikea that you didn't have to put together?

Most of indie music held onto the gritty and the complex against mainstream forms, which, if used at all, were ironically "quoted," but never played seriously. Indie music thought it was *authentic*, not like the *inauthentic* mainstream garbage. An example is the use of lo-fi recording techniques, which were intentionally used to produce a lower recording quality than typical songs. It is like the hipsters' penchant for dumpster-chic; if there is a musical movement associated with the hipster it is certainly indie.

However, it's perfectly possible for a hipster to dislike indie music. They might listen to hip-hop for instance. If punk was mainly white, hip-hop was predominantly black (and, to a lesser degree, Latino). It started in the decaying "nowheres" to which

America had always turned a blind eye: the inner-city ghettos. By the time hip-hop began in the South Bronx and Upper Manhattan in New York City in the 1970s, "inner city" was code for (mostly) black and Latino neighborhoods in dire poverty. For something to do, kids from these neighborhoods began to rap, breakdance, and write graffiti. These were later canonized as the three elements of hip-hop. Unlike punk, hip-hop did not have as much of a problem with commodification; in fact, no other genre of music has celebrated consumerism like hip-hop has.[61] The election of Ronald Reagan in 1980 was experienced as quasi-plague in inner city America. Hip-hop provided the perfect soundtrack to neo-liberalism, the worldwide economic and political system of which Reagan was a part: "Few anticipated either the impact that neoliberalism and hip-hop would have [...] But within a decade hip-hop would be the globally dominant pop music and neoliberalism would have changed the political/economic climate."[62] Hip-hop and neoliberalism both have "an emphasis on 'keeping it real.' Neoliberalism emerged by defining itself against what it labelled as an unrealistic and unsustainable programme of social welfare and public spending." Hip-hop had

> disciplined the looseness of funk, encasing it in the hard snare-drum sound on the Tommy Boy records of the early 1980s. It was as if, under pressure from the newly harsh economic regime – Ronald Reagan came to power in 1981 – the funk body had stiffened into the phallic posturing of the rapper [...] the rapper's eyes were fixed on the street [...] 'street' became code for a contracted sense of reality.

Now, to the main event: *the birth of the hipster.* The origin of the word hipster has its roots in the 1930s/1940s, but the modern hipster began in the mid/late 1980s in New York City.[63] Changes within the now famous Williamsburg, Brooklyn (just across the river from Manhattan) provide a vantage point for tracking larger changes within the hipster. Originally a de-industrialized and impoverished (mainly) Latino neighborhood, artists began to move into the neighborhood in the late 1970's because of cheaper real estate. At the time, living outside the borough of Manhattan was considered to be very *uncool* among the Manhattan crowd. Nevertheless, artists "using their bare hands [...] installed their own plumbing, electrical and sewer lines, and transformed vacant factory floors into a maze of ramshackle bedrooms and airy art studios."[64] However, "the year was circa 1979, and the artists who were the original homesteaders are light years away from the ones making Williamsburg their home today."

Beginning in the 1980s, yuppie mania was sweeping the nation. These "young urban professionals" decided that they did not want to live a dull suburban life; they wanted to live in the big-city. As they moved in, they drove up real estate prices, forcing the creative types (as well as the other people without much money) to move into more marginal neighborhoods, places that were often crime-ridden and clearly less desirable. For many of the older hipsters, the central antagonism (besides hipsters vs. the mainstream) became hipster vs. yuppie (who were always thought to be a part of the mainstream anyway). It is all the more ironic then that these same yuppies would provide fuel for a growing cultural sphere that many hipsters depended on, and have kids that would eventually contribute to the growing hipster population. The traditionally "anti-urban" United States was slowly embracing the urban and was more and more curious as to what was happening in the city. Shows like *Seinfeld*[65], *Friends* and *Sex and the City* (all set in New York City, incidentally) were huge successes: "In the 1990s, major trends of youth fashion – including grunge, hip-hop, and heroin chic – were clearly sold as emerging organically from street culture."[66] In the early '90s, the term hipster "was reborn [...], used again to describe a generation of middle-class youths interested in an alternative art and music scene."[67] There was something different this time though. "Instead of creating a culture of their own, hipsters proved content to borrow from trends long past. Take your grandmother's sweater and Bob Dylan's Wayfarers, add jean shorts, Converse All-Stars and a can of Pabst and bam — hipster." In the mid-1990's their numbers were small but growing, and they were mostly labeled "independent" or "alternative."

The 1990s had "started on a slackerish note, as a generation of Americans was informed it would probably be the first not to match its parents' income. Since the Man was laying everybody off, why not grow a goatee, chase those dreams and forget about growing up and making money?"[68] By the late 1990s the economy picked up and things "played out differently. Real money has found its way to younger and younger people, crashing directly into the postundergrad secondhand-shop lifestyle." The hipster's appearance in the early 1990s, looked at in this light, is no big mystery.

Williamsburg continued to grow. Eve Sussman, a video artist who arrived in Williamsburg in 1992 and counts herself among the second wave of arrivals said "they are cranking them out of the art schools and dropping them on the L train platform. The people who live in Williamsburg now are like the 10th wave [written in 2003]."[69] By the early 2000s the hipster movement had become institutionalized. In Williamsburg, some were "even declaring the [...] scene officially over. In an article written in 2003, a club owner commented 'Williamsburg is definitely no longer underground [...] Six months ago, Williamsburg was terminally hip [...] Now it's become designated as a safe space for nice people who have boring 9 to 5 jobs.'" This was not the first nor would be the last time the hipster was declared dead only to "rise again."

Bands like the Strokes, Modest Mouse, the Decembrists and Franz Ferdinand were part of the mainstreaming of hipsterdom (and "indie" music in general). In fact, indie music (although usually of a "watered down" kind) was quickly becoming the suburban white girl's music of choice. Also beginning in the 2000s was a huge increase in youth listening to classic rock and other older music; perhaps it is a sign of how much things have changed that many would not see this as a big deal, but this evolved as a reaction to the boy/girl band, shiny suit rap era: pure, unabashed corporate trash. The collective delve into the music of their parent's era (and before that) would certainly add many to-be hipsters to the ranks in the future. Often, hipsters went to websites like Pitchfork Media, which became the new trendsetters. It was part of a much larger development, one whose "official" beginning was the "Battle of Seattle", or the 1999 Seattle WTO (World Trade Organization) protests: the "anti-corporate", "anti-globalization" movement. Naomi Klein's popular book *No Logo* examined the effects of the wholesale "branding" of America (and the rest of the capitalist world) since the 1980s when the main mode of advertising became "lifestyle advertising." Advertisers cared less about marketing products; increasingly they were self-consciously selling a certain lifestyle. For example, you weren't just buying Gatorade, you "could be like Mike."[70] While a small part of the movement was anti-capitalist, for the most part the movement was "anti-corporate" and "anti-globalization" (and usually more narrowly anti-branding). In the late 1990s/early-mid 2000s clothing such as American Apparel was laughed out of the mainstream. A little over five years later, it was everywhere.

Contributing to the rise of the hipster was the 2003/2004 technological revolution called Web 2.0. Due to increased Internet bandwidth speeds, information (particularly multi-media information) was easily disseminated. File-sharing became possible on a large scale and applications like Kaaza and Bittorent allowed people to accumulate massive amounts of music, movies, etc. Along with increased internet usage, this had the effect of *devaluing* many types of specialist knowledge. Having good taste was still important, but now anyone could go to a blog with "obscure" music and download "uniqueness." Also, images could be uploaded and shared more easily, giving rise to social-networking sites like MySpace or Facebook. This put an emphasis on the image or the "spectacle." Because vast social-networks were now viewable within a single screen, the drive to present one's self through an *authentic* or *unique* image grew. However, this is not much different from the way that image functions in general within late capitalism:

> the acquisition of an image (by the purchase of a sign system such as designer clothes and the right car) becomes a singularly important element in the presentation of self in labour markets and, by extension, becomes integral to the quest for *individual identity, self-realization, and meaning* [my emphasis].[71]

Although a dated example, "a California firm manufactures imitation car telephones, indistinguishable from the real ones, and they sell like hot cakes to a populace desperate to acquire such a symbol of importance." This MySpace-fueled, image/spectacle-based environment was perfect for the scenester, the less-refined version of the hipster. The scenester aesthetic is an unsavory mix of emo and hipster. Their name designates one of their main characteristics: being down for the "scene" and to be seen, something that they share with hipsters.

After the mid-2000s, the hipster movement exploded. 2007 was a turning point. Before, the hipster was a growing subculture achieving some mainstream recognition; afterwards, the mainstream would be saturated in the hipster aesthetic.[72] The media is currently filled with images of hipsters. Hipsters in advertisements, hipsters on TV shows, hipsters in mainstream movies, etc. It seemed like Hollywood made a collective effort to make the syle of Wes Anderson (hipster/indie filmmaker *extraor-dinaire*) fit for mainstream consumption.

Effects are appearing within other subcultures and, more generally, in pop culture. For example, observe changes within contemporary music. Singers like Lady Gaga and Ke$ha represent the hipster aesthetic filtered through pop culture. In hip-hop, rappers like Kanye West and Lupe Fiasco were, in a way, archetypes of hipster permeation of the larger cultural sphere. Lil' Wayne, arguably the most popular current rapper, embraced Auto-Tune[73] (along with many others), was singing and started playing guitar. Jay-Z in D.O.A. lashes out at this new movement in rap, and is able to condense a couple years of changes within rap in a few short lines, from a "purist" perspective:

> This is anti autotune, death of the ringtone /
> This ain't for iTunes, this ain't for sing alongs…
> You niggas' jeans too tight /
> You colors too bright, your voice too light…
> You niggas singing too much /
> Get back to rap you t-paining too much[74]

It has not only affected rap. The hipster has developed into a more global force, making the different local scenes more uniform. Vice Magazine, a (former?) hipster favorite is a good example of the change: "When the first edition of the glossy freesheet Vice came out in Montreal in 1994, its founders could hardly have believed that, 14 years on, it would be sought out by 900,000 readers on five continents. Now, the Vice empire includes a clothing chain, a record label and an online TV channel. The Vice aesthetic has had an abiding influence on global [hipster] style."[75] Stores like American Apparel and Urban Outfitters expanded rapidly, providing a link from the mall to the street. A good description of the prevailing hipster style (in 2008):

> a speckle of fashion-conscious twentysomethings [although many hipsters are older] hanging about and sporting a number of predictable stylistic trademarks: skinny jeans, cotton spandex leggings, fixed-gear bikes, vintage flannel, fake eyeglasses and a keffiyeh – initially sported by Jewish students and Western protesters to express solidarity with Palestinians, the keffiyeh has become a completely meaningless hipster cliché fashion accessory. The American Apparel V-neck shirt, Pabst Blue Ribbon beer and Parliament cigarettes are symbols and icons of working or revolutionary classes that have been appropriated by hipsterdom and drained of meaning.[76]

Today, it is clear that these symbols of "hipsterdom" are all mainstream staples. The current direction of the hipster seems to be (as if it were in the "nature" of the subculture to do anything else) finding an aesthetic that to the mainstream is even uglier, nerdier; one wonders how long hipsters can "bend the stick" between love of nostalgia (and the infantile) and an equally strong desire for the aged (think of the ridicolous new fashion to wear "grandma" shoes) before it finally breaks.

Notes

1   The following is taken from accounts of Tacitus and Suetonius. Some of the claims in their work have been disputed. While it is possible that this is true of the accounts used here, the purpose of the following is to provide a way to begin understanding the hipster, not an exercise in historiography.

2   Tacitus. *The Annals of Imperial Rome* (London: Penguin, 1996), pg. 320

3 Ibid, pg. 321
4 Ibid, pg. 321
5 Suetonius. *The Twelve Caesars* (London: Penguin, 2007), pg. 222
6 Ibid, pg. 223
7 Maupassant, Guy de. *Bel-Ami.* (New York: Oxford University Press, 2001), pg. 77
8 Ibid, pg. 75
9 Ibid, pg. 76-77
10 Ibid, pg. 77
11 Suetonius. *The Twelve Caesars* (London: Penguin, 2007), pg. 221
12 Ibid, pg. 221-222
13 Ibid, pg. 222
14 Tacitus. *The Annals of Imperial Rome.* (London: Penguin, 1996), pg. 321
15 Rob Walker, "Fauxhemian Rhapsody," *New York Times Magazine,* January 23, 2000, http://www.nytimes.com/2000/01/23/magazine/the-way-we-live-now-1-23-00-fauxhemian-rhapsody.html?pagewanted=3.
16 Hobsbawm, Eric. *The Age of Revolution.* (London: Abacus, 2008), pg. 13
17 Harvey, David. *The Condition of Postmodernity: An Enquiry Into The Origins of Cultural Change.* (Cambridge, USA: Blackwell, 1989), pg. 22
18 Ibid, pg. 22
19 Hobsbawm, Eric. *The Age of Revolution.* (London: Abacus, 2008), pg. 316
20 Lloyd, Richard D. *Neo-Bohemia: Art and Commerce in the Postindustrial City* (New York: Routledge), pg. 49
21 Hobsbawm, Eric. *The Age of Revolution.* (London: Abacus, 2008), pg. 316
22 Lloyd, Richard D. *Neo-Bohemia: Art and Commerce in the Postindustrial City* (New York: Routledge), pg. 49

23 Ibid, pg. 53

24 Hobsbawm, Eric. *The Age of Revolution.* (London: Abacus, 2008), pg. 317

25 Lloyd, Richard D. *Neo-Bohemia: Art and Commerce in the Postindustrial City* (New York: Routledge),, pg. 53

26 Jameson, Fredric. *Jameson on Jameson: conversations on cultural Marxism*; edited by Ian Buchanan. (Durham: Duke University Press, 2007), pg. 77

27 Ibid, pg. 77

28 Harvey, David. *The Condition of Postmodernity: An Enquiry Into The Origins of Cultural Change.* (Cambridge, USA: Blackwell, 1989), pg. 283

29 Badiou, Alain. *The Century* (Cambridge: Polity, 2007), pg. 32-33

30 Ibid, pg. 32-33

31 Ibid, pg. 134

32 Eagleton, Terry. "Capitalism, Modernism and Postmodernism," *New Left Review* 152 (1985): pg. 61

33 Ibid, pg. 67

34 Harvey, David. *The Condition of Postmodernity: An Enquiry Into The Origins of Cultural Change.* (Cambridge, USA: Blackwell, 1989), pg. 22

35 Lloyd, Richard D. *Neo-Bohemia: Art and Commerce in the Postindustrial City* (New York: Routledge), pg. 32

36 Allen Ginsberg, Jack Kerouac, and William S. Burroughs

37 He later identified the voice as William Blake.

38 Meg Wolitzer, "THE NEW SEASON/ART; How the Beat Esthetic Marked Its Time," *New York Times*, September 10, 1995, http://www.nytimes.com/1995/09/10/arts/the-new-seas on-art-how-the-beat-esthetic-marked-its-time.html?page wanted=all.

39 Although, I am not sure if that is how he would refer to it.

40 ("American higher education...suffered a dialectical reversal somewhere around 1980 – to date, the high-water mark of

class mobility in the US – as the universities went from being among the main vehicles of egalitarianism to being the primary means of reproducing class privilege. Everyone talks, with good reason, about the runaway costs of healthcare in the US, but if healthcare inflation since 1980 has exceeded 400 per cent, the price of a university education has risen, on a recent calculation, by an incredible 827 per cent.") Kunkel, Benjamin. "Into the Big Tent." Review of *Valences of the Dialectic*, by Fredric Jameson. *London Review of Books* 32 no. 8 (2010): 12-16, http://www.lrb.co.uk/v32 /n08/benjamin-kunkel/into-the-big-tent

41 With DMT, Buddhism, etc.

42 Again, the divide is not absolute, there being a lot of cross over. The distinction I am setting up is really to be used as a conceptual tool.

43 David Harvey, *The Condition of Postmodernity: An Enquiry Into The Origins of Cultural Change*. (Cambridge, USA: Blackwell, 1989), pg. 38

44 Fredric Jameson, *Postmodernism, or, The Cultural Logic of Late Capitalism*. (Durham: Duke University Press, 1991), pg. xx

45 David Harvey, *The Condition of Postmodernity: An Enquiry Into The Origins of Cultural Change*. (Cambridge, USA: Blackwell, 1989), pg. 44

46 A story about stories, a global or totalizing framework from which to understand the world (two big examples that postmodernism rebelled against: Marxist and Freudian thought).

47 1993 Richard Linklater movie set in 1976 in a high school in the suburbs of Austin, Texas

48 Frederic Jameson, "Five Theses on Marxism," *Monthly Review* (April 1996), 47(11): 1-10.

49 This is not to say that the feminist project is complete (along with many of the other demands of the 1960s)

50 Fredric Jameson, *Postmodernism, or, The Cultural Logic of Late Capitalism*. (Durham: Duke University Press, 1991), pg. 4-5

51 David Harvey, *The Condition of Postmodernity: An Enquiry Into The Origins of Cultural Change*. (Cambridge, USA: Blackwell, 1989), pg. 290 (Even though Paris at the time was over 2.5 million compared to New York's 7 million, per capita, 1980s New York still has more art production)

52 Richard D. Lloyd, *Neo-Bohemia: Art and Commerce in the Postindustrial City* (New York: Routledge), pg. 65

53 David Harvey, *The Condition of Postmodernity: An Enquiry Into The Origins of Cultural Change*. (Cambridge, USA: Blackwell, 1989), pg. 297

54 Ibid, pg. 298

55 Ibid, pg. 163

56 Ibid, pg. 285

57 Ibid, pg. 285

58 Dylan Clark, "The Death and Life of Punk, The Last Subculture." in *The Post-Subcultures Reader*, eds. David Muggleton and Rupert Weinzierl, (Oxford and New York: Berg Publishers, 2004), pg. 223

59 Ibid, pg. 225

60 Unless you are straight edge

61 Ibid, pg. 225

62 E. K. Ritter, "Fact Sheet: Tiger Sharks," *Shark Info*, http://www.sharkinfo.ch/SI4_99e/gcuvier.html

63 Short for independent(ly owned), duhhh (Examples: Sonic Youth, Dinosaur Jr., the Meat Puppets, Husker Du, Pavement)

64 This is not to say that the whole scene was/is like this

65 Mark Fisher, "Mama said knock you out," *New Statesman*, July 2, 2009, http://www.newstatesman.com/music/2009/07/hip-hop-record-rapper

66 There may have been similar scenes, but only New York City could have produced the hipster as he/she is today; New

York City is *the* original hipster mecca. Also, one could argue that the hipster began in the late 1970s.

67 Denny Lee, "Has Billburg Lost Its Cool?" *New York Times*, July 27, 2003, http://www.nytimes.com/2003/07/27/nyregion/has-billburg-lost-its-cool.html?pagewanted=all.

68 In fact, in *Seinfeld* Season Five Episode Three ("The Glasses") Elaine calls Kramer a "hipster-doofus"

69 Richard D. Lloyd, *Neo-Bohemia: Art and Commerce in the Postindustrial City* (New York: Routledge), pg. 244-245

70 Dan Fletcher, "Hipster Subculture Ripe for Parody," *New York Times*, July 29, 2009, http://www.time.com/time/arts/article/0,8599,1913220,00.html

71 Rob Walker, "The Way We Live Now: 1-23-00; Fauxhemian Rhapsody," *New York Times*, January 23, 2000, http://www.nytimes.com/2000/01/23/magazine/the-way-we-live-now-1-23-00-fauxhemian-rhapsody.html? pagewanted=all

72 Denny Lee, "Has Billburg Lost Its Cool?" *New York Times*, July 27, 2003, http://www.nytimes.com/2003/07/27/nyregion/has-billburg-lost-its-cool.html?pagewanted=all

73 Michael Jordan

74 David Harvey, *The Condition of Postmodernity: An Enquiry Into The Origins of Cultural Change.* (Cambridge, USA: Blackwell, 1989), pg. 288

75 There are also countless references to hipsters in popular culture: (for example, just on NBC); In *The Office* Season Seven Episode Five ("The Sting"), Dwight calls Jim a jock-hipster, which Jim of course denies; In *Community* Season One Episode Seventeen the gym teacher calls Jeff a hipster

76 A program that can distort the human voice to sound robotic (but in a human way)

77 Jay-Z, "D.O.A. (Death of Auto-Tune)," 2009, http://www.azlyrics.com/lyrics/jayz/doadeathofautotune.html

78 "Meet the global scenester: He's hip. He's cool. He's everywhere." *The Independent*, August 14, 2008, http://

www.independent.co.uk/life-style/fashion/features/meet-
the-global-scenester-hes-hip-hes-cool-hes-everywhere-
894199.html

Chapter Three

Hipsters and "la passion du réel"

Hipsters are *the* postmodern subculture and are perfect for a culture that has "revolutionized" itself into stasis. The predominant mood is one of "capitalist realism," or "the widespread sense that not only is capitalism the only viable political and economic system, but also that it is now impossible even to imagine a coherent alternative to it."[1] It brings to mind "the phrase attributed to Fredric Jameson and Slavoj Žižek, that it is easier to imagine the end of the world than it is to imagine the end of capitalism." Perhaps a quick glance at Alain Badiou's concept of "la passion du réel," or the passion of the Real, can help in understanding the current cultural impasse.

The passion of the Real (according to Badiou the defining passion of the twentieth century) indicates a tendency for people to strive for authentic, "real" experience and to break up outdated conventions and ways of living. The hipster's passion for the Real is expressed in their longing for authenticity, coupled with nostalgic mania, the mad-dash for the real located in a former time. It goes without saying that, from the beginning, the hipster within late capitalism has been largely defined by the utter fetishization of anything "retro." Consider distressed or worn-out jeans, a trend that arose in Japan, along with other places, in the 1990's, and has since become a dominant trend in mainstream fashion. Japan, in a more accelerated way then its economic counterparts, was a "plastic" society, where "people were starving for the real thing."[2] The "'discovery' of jeans as antiques required a society that could aestheticize the ordinary." Japan was just that society: "it's as if jeans [were] the answer to a society steeped in simulacra." They began to buy vintage jeans (vintage not just in name; some of these jeans were over one-hundred years old) in large numbers at prices ranging from the low hundreds to thousands of dollars.

One could characterize postmodern "contemporary culture as irredeemably historicist, in the bad sense of an omnipresent and indiscriminate appetite for dead styles and fashions [...] for all the styles and fashions of a dead past."[3] Postmodernity wants to have a relationship with the past, but is part of "a new and original historical situation in which we are condemned to seek History by way of our own pop images and simulacra of that history, which itself remains forever out of reach."[4] In these times, "the word *new* doesn't seem to have the same resonance for us any longer; the word itself is no longer new or pristine."[5] In (postmodern) capitalist realism "the focus shifts from the Next Big Thing to the last big thing – how long ago did it happen and just how big was it?"[6]

The hipster and the postmodern share a "penchant for jumbling together all manner of references to past styles [...] Reality, it seems, is being shaped to mimic media images."[7] An "appetite for dead styles and fashions" and a culture increasingly out of touch with history are not opposed but are part of a larger postmodern outlook: "it is safest to grasp the concept of the postmodern as an attempt to think the present historically in an age that has forgotten how to think historically in the first place."[8] Postmodernism "either 'expresses' some deeper irrepressible historical impulse (in however distorted a fashion) or effectively 'represses' and diverts it." It is a paradoxical situation: an age that tries to be in touch with history more than ever, but is more a-historical than ever. This pecularity finds expression in hipsters' love of nostalgia, covering everything from the era of childhood to old age. One gets the feeling that somehow hipsters have, in a move that is not easy on the eyes, found a way to combine these two poles into one general aesthetic. It is like on *Glee*[9] when Kurt points out that somehow "Rachel somehow manages to dress like a grandmother and a toddler at the same time."

"The increasing unavailability of the personal style" in the postmodern era "engendered the well-nigh universal practice today of what may be called *pastiche*."[10] Pastiche, not parody, is a hallmark of the hipster aesthetic (as well as postmodernism in general). In our times parody finds itself without a vocation; it has lived, and that strange new thing pastiche slowly comes to take its place. Pastiche is, like parody, the imitation of a peculiar or unique, idiosyncratic style, the wearing of a linguistic mask, speech in a dead language. But it is a neutral practice of such mimicry, without any of parody's ulterior motives, amputated of the satiric impulse.[11]

Pastiche is parody that is perfect for the age of ironic detachment and cynicism. It is also perfect for an age where the personal and unique style is becoming endangered. Hipsters seem incapable of doing anything creative beyond borrowing from the past, which is part of a more general trend: "the producers of culture have nowhere to turn *but to the past* [my emphasis]: the imitation of dead styles, speech through all the masks and voices stored up in the imaginary museum of a now global culture."[12] Perhaps, by now, the reader has noticed that this chapter and parts of the second chapter are written in what could be called a pastiche style. This is because to critique and understand a certain *zeitgeist* (or worldview), one must think *with*, *against*, and *through* the dominant forms of thought.

Even though the unique style is rapidly disappearing within late capitalism, to some, the fact that it still *persists* is a surprise. In 1936 (in "The Work of Art In The Age Of Mechanical Reproduction") Walter Benjamin already claimed that one could discern "developmental tendencies of art under present conditions of production"[13] that would "brush aside a number of outmoded concepts, such as creativity and genius, eternal value and mystery." While creativity, genius, eternal value and mystery are inseparable from the hipster, Benjamin was addressing his contemporary political situation, his main fear being that these concepts' "uncontrolled [...] application would lead to a processing of data in the Fascist sense." This lead him to the conclusion (still prescient for today) that our "self-alienation has reached such a degree that it can experience its own destruction as an aesthetic pleasure of the first order [movies like *Independence Day* come to mind here?]. This is the situation of politics which Fascism is rendering aesthetic. Communism responds by politicizing art": fascism (or the reactionary) tends to aestheticize the political, while communism (or the revolutionary) tends to politicize the aesthetic. He also introduces his conception of "aura": "that which withers in the age of mechanical reproduction is the aura of the work of art." The decline of aura "is a symptomatic process whose significance points beyond the realm of reproduced object from the domain of tradition."

Tradition is related to "the authenticity of a thing," which "is the essence of all that is transmissible from its beginning, ranging from its substantive duration to its testimony to the history which it has experienced." Also, "the presence of the original is the prerequisite to the concept of authenticity." Benjamin points out that, "in principle a work of art has always been reproducible. Man-made artifacts could always be imitated by men." The age of technical reproduction changes this situation, introduces itself as a historical novelty: "mechanical reproduction of a work of art [...] represents something new." Before technical reproduction, "manual reproduction [...] was usually branded as a forgery [...and] the original preserved all its authority; not so vis-à-vis technical reproduction."

Technical reproduction does not destroy all the authority of the original but drastically reduces it. For example, "the whole sphere of authenticity is outside technical – and, of course, not only technical – reproducibility." Authenticity in this sense can be heavily identified with the one element "the most perfect reproduction of a work of art is lacking [the original's] presence in time and space, its unique existence at the place where it happens to

42

be." No reproduction can claim to have experienced the same history as the original. The importance placed on a certain space and time, or what could be called "the scene," and its connection to "authenticity," clearly resonates among hipsters. Consumer goods, neighborhoods, styles, etc. are fetishized in the cult of "authenticity."

History seems to be moving in the opposite direction of the tendencies that Walter Benjamin perceived:

...for the first time in world history, mechanical reproduction emancipates the work of art from its parasitical dependence on ritual [...] the instant the criterion of authenticity ceases to be applicable to artistic production, the total function of art is reversed. Instead of being based on ritual, it begins to be based on another practice – politics.

In our "apolitical" age this appears to be ridiculous. But today, because of certain socio-economic constraints (the capitalist system for one), art is without a doubt still tied to "ritual," "authenticity," etc.; isn't the hipster a perfect case in point? Benjamin discerned "developmental tendencies of art under present conditions of production" that would "brush aside a number of outmoded concepts, such as creativity and genius, eternal value and mystery." So why have they *not* been "brushed aside," and in particular, *why do they still live on in hipsters?* Why do the "originals" still preserve their authority, or at least emit an "aura" of excessive fascination? What is with the nostalgic backs-liding?

Through nostalgia, hipsters can express their passion for the Real by being "unique" and "authentic". It is important to keep in mind that the "original" hipsters in the 1980s/1990s (although it continues into the 2000s) were going against a mainstream culture that valued placed an emphasis on the "new." In consuming "retro," they are, in their minds, going against the mainstream and being "authentic" by resisting commodification's relentless outpouring of "new" products. In pursuing "authenticity," they are exploring territory familiar to many of the predecessor groups discussed in Chapter Two, as well as to the passion for the real. "There exists a passion for the real that is obsessed with identity: to grasp real identity, to unmask its copies, to discredit fakes. It is a passion for the authentic, and authenticity is in fact a category that belongs to Heidegger as well as to Sartre,"[14] who provided the philosophical post-war counterculture. The passion for the real in the mode of authenticity "can only be fulfilled as destruction. Herein lies its strength – after all, many things deserve to be destroyed. But this is also its limit, because purification is a process doomed to incompletion, a figure of the bad infinite." Countercultures based on the notion of authenticity have tried to resist the mainstream by simply negating it: if they do this, then we do the opposite. The problem with this strategy is that it does not set up anything in the place of what it opposes and creates the cycle of "bad infinity." "Authenticity" requires "destroy[ing] every density, every claim to substantiality, and every assertion of reality."[15] This is why "the [20th] century attempts to react against depth. It carries out a fierce critique of foundations and of the beyond; it promotes the immediate, as well as the surface of sensation." The hipster is a sign that "authenticity" as a mode of resistance no longer works. The result is that the hipster aesthetic exhibits a "new kind of flatness or depthlessness, a new kind of superficiality in the most literal sense" which is "perhaps the supreme formal feature of all the postmodernisms."[16] The reaction against depth produced a characteristic effect of postmodern culture: "an effacement of the older distinction between high and so-called mass culture."[17] The hipster, in typical postmodern fashion, has no problem with dabbling in pop culture. It may seem that the hipsters still remains within the frame of modernism, which relied upon the distinction between high and low culture, "its

44

Utopian function consisting at least in part in the securing of a realm of *authentic experience* [my emphasis] over against the surrounding environment of middle-brow and low-brow commercial culture." In the face of a homogenizing "culture industry," one could seek solace in knowing they did not listen to the same music or read the same books as "everybody else." However, the hipster is *within* the postmodern outlook. Instead of authentic experience being outside of "middle-brow and low-brow commercial culture," as in modernism, the postmodern hipster's quest for authenticity is firmly bound up with it. That being said, the distinction high/low remains and has shifted. Instead of being about what products one consumes, the emphasis has shifted to *how* one is consuming the products (i.e. "we may be consuming the same products, but my experience is *more authentic* than yours") and an elitist outlook remains. It is no coincidence that this is also part of the dominant mode of marketing (part of the shift responsible for "lifestyle advertising") within postmodern capitalism

> where at the level of consumption, this new spirit is that of so-called 'cultural capitalism': we primarily buy commodities neither on account of their utility nor as status symbols [or the older predominant forms of marketing]; we buy them to get the experience provided by them, we consume them in order to render our lives pleasurable and meaningful.[18]

Ultimately the passion for the real concerns itself with the "(re)commencement of Man: the new man."[19] This can take on two different meanings. "For a whole host of thinkers, particularly in the area of fascist thought (and without excepting Heidegger), 'the new man' is in part the restitution of the man of old, of the man who had been eradicated, had disappeared, had been corrupted." The process of purification then is "the more or less violent process of the return of a vanished origin. The new is a production of authenticity." It is easy to see then, how the "restitution (of the origin) through destruction (of the inauthentic)" corresponds to the hipster's love of nostalgia. What is beyond the scope of the hipster imagination is the idea of the new man as a "real creation, something that has never existed before, because he emerges from the destruction of historical antagonisms." This is a new man who "is beyond classes and beyond the state." This "truly" new man would therefore smash the kind of distinctions that the hipster's elitist outlook, a curious "self-denying" elitism, depends on. While the hipster circulates endlessly in a wheel of bad infinity, the idea of a truly new humanity hangs in the balance.

Garbage, The Sacred Place, and the Hipster Aesthetic

The never-ending imperative to accumulate profits created twin processes, "the progressive commodification of aesthetics and the aesthetification of the universe of commodities."[20] Aesthetics has become more tied to the structure of commodities, while commodities have become more "beautiful" (or aesthetically pleasing). Who wouldn't want to make their products look better? Wouldn't most people choose the "beautiful" product over the "ugly" or "non-descript" product? *Not hipsters.* They are tired of the too beautiful, overly perfect "mainstream" culture and face the same problem that modern/postmodern art has been dealing with for decades: how to maintain the Sacred Place (the Void) against relentless commodification. In a society based on the commodity form (or capitalism) "the profound vocation of the work of art in a commodity society" is *"not to be a commodity, not to be consumed, to be unpleasurable* in the commodity sense."[21] The Sacred Place then is that "of the central Void, the empty ('sacred') place of the Thing exempted from the circuit of everyday economy, which is then filled in by a positive object that is thereby 'elevated to the dignity of the Thing'."[22] More bluntly, in this case, it is a "beautiful" object (one with the ability to inspire awe) because it is something that has little immediate "use" or "exchange" value.

The Sacred Place is coming under attack: "today, the true pieces of trash are the 'beautiful' objects with which we are constantly bombarded from all sides," (for example, Victoria Secret commercials) which means that, for the hipster (and other postmodernists), "the only way to escape trash is to put *trash itself* into the sacred place of the Void."[23] Hipsters' love of "garbage-dump chic" (or whatever is perceived to be less "aesthetically pleasing") is now cast in a different light. What seems like garbage is "elevated into a work of art, used to fill in the Void of the Thing...not simply to demonstrate that 'anything goes', that the object is ultimately irrelevant...but to ascertain that the Sacred Place is still there."[24] Hipsters, "far from undermining the logic of sublimation, are desperately striving to *save* it."[25] So if the problem of traditional (premodern) art was how to fill in the sublime Void of the Thing (the pure Place) with an adequately beautiful object...the problem of modern art is [...] no longer that [...] of filling in the Void, but, rather, that of *creating* the Void in the first place.[26]

Facing a "too aestheticized," "too commodified" world, the hipster holds on to the Sacred Place by clutching on to what seem to be pieces of "trash." Meaning has reduced to a place within relatively "meaningless" objects.

However, things are a little more complex for the hipster: capitalist consumerism is no longer just a conformity machine:

It's as if the era of mass production and mass culture has now yielded not standardization, but a proliferation of difference, of otherness. Corporations don't advertise to a mass public any more. It's now niche advertising - addressing the subtle differentiation between one consumer public and another, exploiting cultural fragmentation.[27]

Capitalism is able to sell either "mainstream" notions of beauty or notions of beauty that are held by a small-niche group; whatever makes the most profits will be sold. Hipsters today have to deal with a process of commodification that not only tries to standardize, but embraces the logic of "difference" and "uniqueness." This means that putting "garbage" in the Sacred Place is not enough to save it: for example, last years' unsellable, hideous piece of clothing (the kind that hipsters would fetishize) becomes this years' hot new item. Trucker hats, which became widespread among hipsters in the early 2000s, were such an item. What was once an extremely "uncool" and "lower class" thing to wear became a hipster sensation. Then, suddenly, they hit the mainstream: picture every star from Paris Hilton to Dennis Rodman in their overpriced Von Dutch trucker hat.

The hipster aesthetic can perhaps be best understood through Susan Sontag's notion of camp. "Camp is a certain mode of aestheticism. It is one way of seeing the world as an aesthetic phenomenon...not in terms of beauty, but in terms of the degree of artifice, of stylization."[28] In fact the essence of camp is "its love of the unnatural: of artifice and exaggeration. And Camp is esoteric — something of a private code, a badge of identity even, among small urban cliques," perhaps among groups such as hipsters. By love of exaggeration Sontag means "the 'off,' of things-being-what-they-are-not."

Doesn't the love of "exaggeration" and "artifice" that Sontag describes go against striving for authenticity? They seem to be completely opposed, but they mark the end points of the hipster continuum. The "authentic" side (perhaps best represented in the mainstream by American Apparel) features the stripped-down, non-commercial/no-logo, faux working class hipster. At the other end, the "artificial" side (for a mainstream example perhaps Urban Outfitters) represents the kind of hipster who is saturated in artifice, irony; a good example is a 'sneaker-freak,' or the kind of person who would own ten different pairs of Jordans (usually running over $100 each). Jeff Winger's description of Abed in *Community* (Season Two Episode Nineteen) nicely encapsulates the attitude of the 'artificial' hipster:

> His obsession with pop culture had always alienated him. He'd quote movies, pretend his life was a TV show, he watched Cougartown...it was as if he didn't want people to like him.[29]

In reality, hipsters embody both extremes. It is crucial to note that even if they are ever so slight, the "authentic" and "artificial" sides are embodied within each hipster, otherwise they would cease to be a hipster.

Going back to "Camp," Sontag gives us the "formal" key to understanding hipsters' endless nostalgic consumerism:

> This is why so many of the objects prized by Camp taste are old-fashioned, out- of-date, démodé. It's not a love of the old as such. It's simply that the process of aging or deterioration provides the necessary detachment — or arouses a necessary sympathy.[30]

The essence of the hipster, then, is a detachment from this reality, a refusal to be fully complicit with what is going on now. The hipster attempts to preserve their individuality by negating the world around it. *The passion for the Real turns into its opposite, a denial of reality.* "When the theme is important, and contemporary, the failure of a work of art may make us indignant. Time can change that. Time liberates the work of art from moral relevance, delivering it over to the Camp sensibility." Hipsters do not seem to have nostalgia for the "recent" past because it is still too visible, still too present (think about hipster's love of Polaroids and other old photographs, viewing the current situation through the nostalgic gaze). One wonders if this has anything to do with the fact that "detachment is the prerogative of an elite; and as the dandy is the 19th century's surrogate for the aristocrat in matters of culture, so Camp is the modern dandyism. Camp is the answer to the problem: how to be a dandy in the age of mass culture." So perhaps then, being a hipster is the answer to the problem of how to be a dandy in our age. It is the imaginary resolution to a real problem: how one can meld rebellion, which draws energies from the lower classes, with an elite sensibility:

> At its best the hipster is the new Dandy, the semi-subversive who overloads the system by over-subscribing to it (conspicuously consuming) and yet undermines it by seeming as if the real source of their cooperation is that they can't take the system seriously enough to bother to oppose it.[31]

It is not hard to see that the dominant political expression among hipsters seems to be a noxious mixture of libertarianism and apathy, *an appropriate mix for the neo-liberal era*. Why bother to fight the system when one can remain safely in the margins (so that the basic running of things is left undisturbed)?

Why Hipsters Don't Call Themselves Hipsters

It seems to be common knowledge, at least among those that would be considered hipsters, that today, authenticity is a fiction. After seeing the previous subcultures that carried the banner of authenticity fail time and time again (and continue to be co-opted by the system), hipsters seem to "know" the authenticity game is over with late-multinational-postmodern capitalism. So *why, in their actions, do they still pursue authenticity?*

Can this possibly have anything to do with the fact that hipsters usually do not recognize themselves as hipsters? Ask any hipster if they are, in fact, a hipster, and one usually get an emphatic "No!" or an inquiry into the validity of the question itself ("what really *is* a hipster?") The hipster is everyone else, never oneself. Everything seems shrouded in mystery, including how denial has become the new standard.

Slavoj Žižek's work on ideology helps to illuminate what is going on here. His basic thesis is that the traditional notion of ideology as false consciousness ("they don't know what they are doing") is no longer tenable today. The idea behind the false consciousness theory of ideology is that once people find out what the "facts" are they will rise up in revolution against the system that oppresses them. Nike provides an example. Before the public found out that Nike was using sweatshop labor, one could have said that people buying Nike shoes were under "false consciousness" because they were not aware that teenage girls in Asia are making their shoes for a couple cents an hour. However, the public did eventually find out about this and people kept buying Nike shoes. So clearly ideology is not just a matter of "not knowing" what is going on. While the notion of "false consciousness" is not completely obsolete, today's ideology, Žižek claims, runs more on the idea that "they know very well what they are doing, but they continue to do it anyway." Žižek's anecdote about Niels Bohr, famous quantum physicist, helps clarify the nature of contemporary ideology:

> ...surprised at seeing a horseshoe above the door of Bohr's country house, the fellow scientist visiting him exclaimed that he did not share the superstitious belief regarding horseshoes keeping evil spirits out of the house, to which Bohr snapped back: 'I don't believe in it either. I have it there because I was told that it works even when one doesn't believe in it:' This is indeed how ideology functions today: nobody takes democracy or justice seriously, we are all aware of their corrupted nature, but we participate in them, we display our belief in them, because we assume that they work even if we do not believe in them.[32]

Ideology no longer requires conscious "belief"; belief is shown through one's actions. You may not "believe" in democracy, but if you still vote, then through your actions you are indicating that you *really do* believe. This is how the *cynical* mode of ideology functions. It claims, incorrectly, to have "delivered us from the 'fatal abstractions' inspired by the 'ideologies of the past,'"[33] protecting "us from the perils posed by belief itself." It is part of "the attitude of ironic distance [no stranger to hipsters] proper to postmodern capitalism," which "is supposed to immunize us against the seductions of fanaticism. Lowering our expectations, we are told, is a small price to pay for being protected from terror and totalitarianism." It is part of the atmosphere of "capitalist realism," which is not "confined to art or to the quasi-propagandistic way in which advertising functions,"[34] but "is more like a pervasive atmosphere, conditioning not only the production of culture but also the regulation of work and education, and acting as a kind of invisible barrier constraining thought and action." In this environment, "Really Existing Capitalism is marked by the same division which characterized Really Existing Socialism [the name for the shitty pseudo-socialism of the twentieth century] [...] On the one hand, [there is] an official culture in which capitalist enterprises are presented as socially responsible and caring, and, on the other, a widespread awareness that companies are actually corrupt, ruthless, etc."[35]

All of this applies to the hipster. They know very well that the concept of authenticity is a lie (in that it is no longer a viable mode of resistance), but their actions indicate otherwise. In step with the cynical mode of ideology today, hipsters do not need to "consciously" believe that they are hipsters for the system to function. Perhaps this is why they do not call themselves hipsters: in calling someone a hipster, it is uncomfortably bearing witness to the fact that their quest for authenticity is a failed one from the start; it is pointing out that they are not "unique" and are like all the other hipsters. A subculture that seeks to go beyond labels will of course react viciously to being labeled.

Hipsters stick to the idea of being authentic self-creators, not because they are stupid and do not know any better, but because it is a necessary illusion within our current system. Being an authentic self-creator has become our culture's predominant *fundamental fantasy*. The Lacanian meaning of fundamental fantasy is a story created by a subject "which gives his or her life a perception of consistency and stability, while he or she also perceives the social order as being coherent and not marked by antagonisms."[36] It is the subject's primary stance towards the world. Also, "in order to be operative, fantasy has to remain 'implicit', it has to maintain a distance towards the explicit symbolic texture sustained by it, and to function as its inherent transgression."[37] If a hipster is identified as such, it disrupts the whole fantasy. Important within the Lacanian notion of fantasy is its intersubjective component...What?

Hipsters, along with much of contemporary culture, have not dug deep inside themselves to find that they want to be authentic self-creators; rather, they try to be authentic self-creators because they believe that this is what others *want them to do*. Fantasy is a way of temporary solving "the original question of desire," which "is not directly 'What do I want?, but 'What do *others* want from me? What do they see in me? What am I to others?'"[38] Therefore, "at its most fundamental, fantasy tells me what I am to my others." A good example of fantasy's intersubjective character is reported by Freud, of his little daughter fantasizing about eating a strawberry cake:

...what we have here is by no means the simple case of the direct hallucinatory satisfaction of a desire (she wanted a cake, didn't get it, so she fantasized about it). The crucial feature is that, while voraciously eating a strawberry cake, the little girl noticed how her parents were deeply satisfied by seeing her fully enjoying it. What the fantasy of eating a strawberry cake really was about was her attempt to form such an identity (of the one who fully enjoys eating a cake given by the parents) that would satisfy her parents and make her the object of their desire.[39]

If "fantasy is essentially a lure that conceals the subject's mainspring, masking what truly makes the subject 'tick,'"[40] then what is the fantasy of an "authentic self-creator" masking? What is it about contemporary culture that seems to demand "authentic self-creators?"

First, the economy has seen an increase in the number of creative jobs as the cultural sphere has expanded within postmodern late capitalism. However many of these jobs can be just as corporatized and constraining as typical "cubicle work." Also, there are those that seek to be in the culture industry but have to take a part or full time job to allow them to continue their art (such as being a waitress or bartender). The hipster aesthetic, or the idea of being an authentic self-creator more generally, is a way for the growing "creative proletariat" to compensate for the fact that their work is neither creative nor fulfilling.

Second, in general, the economy has seen a downturn in lifetime employment as people now go from career to career throughout their life, making many lifelong "free-lancers." The traditional insecurities associated with bohemia have been dispersed throughout much of the working sector. In late capitalism,

> ...forgetting becomes an adaptive strategy [...] this strategy – of accepting the incommensurable and the senseless without question – has always been the exemplary technique of sanity as such, but it has a special role to play in late capitalism, that 'motley painting of everything that ever was', whose dreaming up and junking of social fictions is nearly as rapid as its production and disposal of commodities.[41]

The instabilities that used to be associated with the realm of the lower classes have crept up behind the middle class, who is rapidly disappearing. "Only a certain kind of human being can prosper in [the current] unstable, fragmentary social conditions...If institutions no longer provide a long-term frame, the individual may have to improvise his or her life-narrative, or even do without any sustained sense of self."[42] This narrative, or fundamental fantasy, is of course that of the authentic self-creator.

Third, the economy of late capitalism requires a lot of "free labor." Free labor is "a specific trait of the cultural economy at large, an important, and yet undervalued force in advanced capitalist societies."[43] The Internet is an example of something that is maintained through gigantic amounts of free labor. Take Facebook for instance. One may be having fun posting pictures and stating one's likes and dislikes (in fact having fun is a key part of the process), but this trivial enjoyment is set against a larger backdrop: Facebook has become one of the largest data mines in the world. Companies love accessing it to find out consumer's tastes, porn websites have been known to take Facebook pictures for use on their own websites, and so on. To feed its inherently-ever-growing appetite for profit, capitalism always seeks to extend the working-day; every last second of free time is squeezed into the profit machine. So Facebook, maintained by countless hours of "free labor," is now part of the machinery of the system.

Within late capitalism a lot of "free labor" could be classified as *immaterial labor,* a concept that is becoming more and more important. Immaterial labor "is defined as the labor that produces the informational and cultural content of the commodity."[44] The latter, the cultural content of a commodity, is more relevant to the topic at hand. In the producing the cultural content of a content of commodity, immaterial labor "involves a series of activities that are not normally recognized as 'work' —

in other words, the kinds of activities involved in defining and fixing cultural and artistic standards, fashions, tastes, consumer norms, and, more strategically, public opinion." Therefore, immaterial labor in this sense could be something as simple as arguing with your friend over which band is better. Or, take the once dominant trend in hip-hop/inner-city culture of having baggy clothing (and perhaps boots like Timberlands). Rappers usually derive their style from what they see the drug dealers wearing. Drug dealers happened to wear baggy clothes because it was easier to, for example, hide things while having on two or three pairs of pants so that they cops would not be able to find them on the "pat-down." Also multiple layers of clothing and boots allowed one to stay warm in the cold, out hustling all night. What was more a matter of utility became a fashion statement. Rappers (many of whom used to be "in the street") who wanted to project a tough image borrowed from the styles of street soldiers. Eventually, the system was able to take this immaterial labor, commodify it, sell it worldwide and reap the profits. Or, as another example, owners of "hip" art galleries that know most (around 90%) of the "hip" looking people in the gallery are not interested in purchasing artwork, but encourage them to come anyway, so as to give off a good appearance. *This is why it is wrong to see those who do not succeed within (neo)-bohemia (the overwhelming majority) as "unnecessary" to the scene. In fact the opposite is true: without the "posers" or the "dilettantes," there would be no scene.* Hopefully this helps illustrate the notion that immaterial knowledge "is inherently collective [and] is even more so in the case of the postmodern cultural economy: music, fashion, and information are all produced collectively but are selectively compensated." As Adorno rightly pointed out (in talking about music), "dilettantism is nothing but the echo and the degenerate product of the true music-making tradition. It remains to be asked for whom the last artist will meaningfully play once the last dilettante who still dreams of being an artist has died out."[45] And, of course, not all the participants are compensated. The profits instead mostly go to the companies that have "privatized" this "general intellect."[46] Another example from the origins of "distressed jeans" shows "immaterial labor" that has been privatized.

> This is how 'vintage' jeans happen: Troy Pierce buys a pair of new Levi's and wears them six days a week for more than a year. He rides his motorcycle in them, commuting from his place in Williamsburg to work in SoHo. He eats his Subway lunch on them. He works in them, loafs in them, D.J.'s in them. And he washes them, in cold water by hand, but only twice.[47]

Then comes along "Sun Choe, a Levi's designer from San Francisco" who stops by the store where Troy works. "Choe likes the look of the grimy life contained in Troy's jeans so much that she wants to make a copy of them, distressed in exactly the same way that his jeans are – with identical 3-D 'whisker' folds below the front pockets, fades along the thighs and that shredded back pocket." Troy refused at first, but then finally consented. The jeans were later taken to a lab to be tested and researched so that exact copies could be made. Hipsters are an integral part of this process. Being cool takes a lot of labor, immaterial labor. Hipsters are part of the laboratory of fashions and tastes which designers can then expropriate for their own benefit. The hipster's cultural imperialism gets turned back against itself.

It should not be hard then to make the connections between a growing urban real estate market, that is both central to late capitalism and operates largely on the concept of selling the "authentic" urban life, and the growth of hipsterdom. Hipsters are part of a larger process of making neighborhoods "cool" or "authentic." Their immaterial labor helps to keep the gentrification machine rolling, a situation rife with irony because from day one the yuppie-gentrifier has been one of the hipster's greatest enemies. The consumption of "authenticity" within real estate fits nicely with the dominant mode of advertising/ consumption today: a product providing a "meaningful" and "authentic" experience. So capitalism, "at the level of consumption, integrated the legacy of '68, the critique of alienated consumption" by learning that "authentic experience matters. A recent Hilton Hotels publicity campaign consists of a simple claim: 'Travel doesn't only get us from place A to place B. It should also make us a better person."[48] In pursuing authenticity, the hipster is perfectly in line with the dominant mode of consumption.

So, in the end, hipsters are not that much different from mainstream society. Many would quickly counter that there is no "mainstream," just a bunch of subcultures. This is correct except that "the bunch of subcultures" IS the mainstream today. The mainstream is now more "de-centered" than it was in the past; there are more than five channels on TV, there is more niche marketing etc. The lack of a "dominant center" within the mainstream does not mean that the mainstream is dead: the *form* of the mainstream has changed. "Mediators" between the different sections of the mainstream are increasingly necessary in today's world. Hipsters desire to be invisible mediators:

This formula, 'include me out', provides the most succinct definition of the *obsessional's* subjective attitude. That is to say: what is the goal of the obsessional attitude? To achieve the position of a pure invisible mediator – that is, to play, in intersubjective relations, the role of what, in chemistry, one calls a 'catalyst': the substance which speeds up, or even sets in motion, a process of chemical reaction without itself changing or being affected in any way.[49]

And increasingly, while "mediators" are needed to link up the disparate zones within the mainstream, there has been a general decline in "craftsmanship," or "learning to do just one thing really well."[50] "Craftsmanship sits uneasily in the institutions of flexible capitalism,"[51] or late capitalism. "The problem lies in...doing something for its own sake. The more one understands how to do something well, the more one cares about it." However, in late capitalism, which is "based on short-term transactions and constantly shifting tasks [...management] can fear it; the management code word here is *ingrown*." "Such commitment can often prove economically destructive. In place of craftsmanship, modern culture advances an idea of meritocracy which celebrates potential ability rather than past achievement."[52] The decline of craftsmanship in the workplace has seeped into the cultural realm, but the hipster's aesthetic, or at least in its more "gritty" varieties, seems to oppose this by fetishizing the look of the lower classes, or the types of people who are more likely to have a gritty aesthetic which shows the rugged nature of their craftsmanship. Again, vintage jeans provide an excellent example:

> Vintage jeans aren't supposed to be polished, high-grade antiques. They're supposed to suggest a life that – from the looks of it – has you crawling around on your knees, crouching for long periods of time and smearing your thighs with your life's dirt. "People spend too much time in sterile environments, " Gregory, the jeans designer, says. "They get up, go to the gym and the office, and they move from one air-conditioned room to another. People are into the authenticity of vintage jeans because they don't want to look like they spend all day at a computer."[53]

The image of a craftsman that the hipster tries to portray is typically a false one and is part of the misdirected passion for the real. It is also artificial because the hipster is marked by an *absence* of craftsmanship: in most cases hipsters just want to dabble and play, being committed is passé.

One could look at the hipster as the *diet-Coke* subculture, in step with our postmodern world. The marketplace is full of "product[s] deprived of [their] substance... in the way decaffeinated coffee smells and tastes like the real coffee without being the real one."[54] Hipsters are counter-culture deprived of its substance; their revolt has no substantial basis except in superficial revolt itself: "is this not the attitude of today's hedonistic Last Man? Everything is permitted, you can enjoy everything, BUT deprived of its substance which makes it dangerous." They appropriate rough and dirty immaterial labor and tack it to themselves like stars you get on your 2nd grade notebook, but do not seem to care much about the toil and sweat that went into the aesthetic they steal. Spreading all over our postmodern culture, the *diet-Coke* logic has gone hand-in-hand with today's dominant ideology of clean capitalism. Many of the current elites fashion themselves as world saviors, while playing the populist card. Marx, today widely (and falsely) considered to be outdated, denounced this hypocritical stance over 100 years ago, when he noted that these "humanitarian" hearts seem to be extracted from the those that they oppress:

> You may be a model citizen, perhaps a member of the Society for the Prevention of Cruelty to Animals, and in the odour of sanctity to boot; but the thing that you represent face to face with me has no heart in its breast. That which seems to throb there is my own heart-beating.[55]

Hipsters are participants in the dominant ideology that "combines pleasure with constraint [which] is no longer the old notion of the right measure' between pleasure and constraint, but a kind of pseudo-Hegelian immediate coincidence of the opposites: action and reaction should coincide." Consumption patterns have become increasingly based on this logic. Buying things (traditionally thought to be "bad" consumerism) is slowly becoming an exercise in social responsibility (such as the hype surrounding organic foods). Today,

> ...consumption is supposed to sustain the quality of life, its time should be "quality time" - not the time of alienation, of imitating models imposed by society, of the fear of not being able to 'keep up with the Joneses;' but the time of the authentic fulfilment of my true Self, of the sensuous play of experience, and of caring for others, through becoming involved in charity or ecology, etc.[56]

Another "coincidence of the opposites" can be found in the dominant consumption patterns of 1990's/2000's America: big box stores, like Walmart, and "luxury" items, like Starbucks coffee. The hipster not only combines an elite sensibility with an aesthetic largely derived from the "lower classes" (like the afromentioned problem of how to be a dandy in our age: how one can meld rebellion, which draws energies from the oppressed, with an elite sensibility). It also attempts to present a (false) aesthetic solution to a real problem: how to unify an increasingly fragmented working class, which is

> split into three, each fraction with its own 'way of life' and ideology: the enlightened hedonism and liberal multiculturalism of the intellectual class; the populist fundamentalism of the old working class; more extreme and singular forms of the outcast fraction.[57]

While the hipster seems to be the aesthetic ideology of the "intellectual class," its influence has spread to the other realms of the social sphere.

Rather than be *flexible*, hipsters should embrace *plasticity*. For Catherine Malabou, plasticity is the ability of the brain "to receive a form or impression" *and* the ability to give form.[58] It follows from what should be a relatively obvious insight: we have the ability *to react upon* and *to be reacted upon by* our environment. What defines the hipster is *flexibility*, or the way that the dominant discourse defines plasticity. Flexibility is *only* the ability to receive form, i.e. it lacks to ability of autoformation. The difference between *plasticity* and *flexibility* is, very simply, the difference between those who can successfully react upon and change the underlying structure of their environment and those who are tools, merely replicating it.

How do hipsters relate (and replicate) the problems that Slavoj Žižek enumerated as antagonisms to the reproduction of the liberal-capitalist system (as well as global capitalism)? The four antagonisms are the looming threat of an ecological catastrophe; the inappropriateness of the notion of private property in relation to so-called "intellectual property" ; the socio ethical implications of new techno-scientific developments (especially in biogenetics); and, last but not least, the creation of new forms of apartheid, new Walls and slums.[59]

Faced with ecological catastrophe, hipsters offer up a model of "sustainable living" that quickly turns into its opposite. Hipsters may oppose intellectual property (although it without a doubt has its supporters), but they're revolt is just negation (they have not yet grasped negation of the negation). Even if they protest, most have not grasped the root of the problem. In regards to new techno-scientific developments, the hipster embraces what could be called an "Avatar" model. The movie *Avatar*'s storyline demands a fantastical rendering, like its choice of a lush digital-panacea chic (merely the flipside of gritty hipster cyberpunk disutopia?). The Na'vi (or the supposed natives), in fact, seem to be a postmodern leftist's greatest utopian dream: they are a people (1) that are supposed to be one with nature (so much so that their environment is part of a large spirit, which they can "plug into"), a stance intended to please environmentalists, (2) that are pre-modern (if we understand modernism to be the process of industrial capitalism), which offers a nod to supporters of a return back to nature, such as Evo Morales (who has publicly supported the movie) to those advocating de-industrialization all the way to adherents of anarcho-primi-vistism, (3) that are placed, paradoxically, within the frame of our postmodern digital fantasy today, on the one hand embracing the idea of the multitude and the hope that we will be able to upload our souls onto some sort network (they are able to plug in and channel the flow of the multitude (Hardt and Negri), showing that the "capitalist" multitude masks the fact that the "one" is growing stronger (through larger, more monopolistic corporate control over life and in the movie where the Na'vi still have centralized authority)), and (4) that are supposed to be in touch with their "spiritual" side, something that will likely appeal to mystical new-agers and the like. This combination is unworkable even in theory: most hipsters, like a lot of dominant mainstream attitudes today, haved not yet arrived at the idea that the only way to solve the threat of ecological collapse is *by using science.* In regards to the fourth, and most important, antagonism, the division of excluded and included, *the hipster, while sporting the aesthetic of the oppressed, is clearly on the elite side.* Perhaps the most general feature of the hipster's subjectivity is "the fear of 'excessive' identification [...], the fundamental feature of the late- capitalist ideology: the Enemy is the 'fanatic' who 'overidentifies' instead of maintaining a proper distance toward the dispersed plurality of subject-positions."[60] The frequent depiction of hipsters as people whose manufactured ennui prevents them from seriously identifying with something is true. This is supposed to be going against the current order. However "far from containing any kind of subversive potentials, the dispersed, plural, constructed subject hailed by postmodern theory (the subject prone to particular, inconsistent modes of enjoyment, etc.) simply designates *the form of subjectivity that corresponds to late capitalism.*" What seems to be fighting the system (if hipsters even have time to care) only sustains it. So,

> perhaps the time has come to resuscitate the Marxian insight that Capital is the ultimate power of 'deterritorialization' which undermines every fixed social identity, and to conceive of 'late capitalism' as the epoch in which the traditional fixity of ideological positions (patriarchal authority, fixed sexual roles, etc.) becomes an obstacle to the unbridled commodification of everyday life.

To properly oppose the system, hipsters do not need to try to *merely* disrupt the current social landscape, because capitalism does this anyway. It is time to think overturning the process of disruption itself and instituting an economy with *real* democracy (democratic control of the workplace and the economy as a whole), not just a consumer's democracy (which can be as democratic as elections in a totalitarian state).

Some have said the spread of the hipster is part of the breakdown of Western Civilization. This view, while prescient in the light of a worldwide current ecological crisis that could launch humanity into barbarism (possibly wiping out all mankind), is perhaps a bit too catastrophic. The hipster does not represent absolute evil, but a pathetic attempt (like much of postmodernism) to bring a cynical-utopia into the (late-) capitalism world. There is plenty of room for pessimism, but there are bright spots on the horizon. Consider Hegel's view of repetition in history. After a truly historical break, say the advent of a new art form, continuing to repeat the past as if the event has not happened leads to kitsch (as exemplified in the hipster aesthetic), it no longer sounds the same. Ironically, this failure to repeat the past eventually leads to something new. Hipsters can attempt to be as "authentic" and "original" as much as they like: they are only clearing the ground for something new and world changing. In the mean time, for those intentionally trying to change the world for the better, authenticity as a mode of resistance should be abandoned. We have the ability to break the cycle of "bad infinity." It is time to do what has always been called impossible: the creation of a "truly" new man through the creation of a society without classes. Any other solution simply will not suffice.

Notes

1   Mark Fisher, *Capitalist Realism: Is There No Alternative?*, (Zer0 Books: Winchester, UK, 2009), pg. 2

2   Austin Bunn, "Not Fade Away," *New York Times*, December 1, 2002, http://www.nytimes.com/2002/12/01/magazine/not-fade-away.html?pagewanted=all

3   Fredric Jameson, *Postmodernism, or, The Cultural Logic of Late Capitalism*. (Durham: Duke University Press, 1991), pg. 286

4   Ibid, pg. 25

5   Ibid, pg. 310

6   Mark Fisher, *Capitalist Realism: Is There No Alternative?*, (Zer0 Books: Winchester, UK, 2009), pg. 3

7   David Harvey, *The Condition of Postmodernity: An Enquiry Into The Origins of Cultural Change*. (Cambridge, USA: Blackwell, 1989), pg. 85

8   Fredric Jameson, *Postmodernism, or, The Cultural Logic of Late Capitalism*. (Durham: Duke University Press, 1991), pg. IX

9   *Glee* S01E11; by the way, *Glee*, a story about the outcasts overcoming the odds, is a perfect story for the age of hipster

10   Fredric Jameson, *Postmodernism, or, The Cultural Logic of Late Capitalism*. (Durham: Duke University Press, 1991), pg. 16

11   Ibid, pg. 17

12   Ibid, pg. 17-18

13   Walter Benjamin, "The Work Of Art In The Age Of Mechanical Reproduction," http://marxists.org/reference/subject/philosophy/works/ge/benjamin.htm

14 Alain Badiou, *The Century* (Cambridge: Polity, 2007), pg. 56

15 Ibid, pg. 64

16 Fredric Jameson, *Postmodernism, or, The Cultural Logic of Late Capitalism.* (Durham: Duke University Press, 1991), pg. 9

17 Ibid, pg. 63

18 Slavoj Žižek, *First as Tragedy Then as Farce,* (New York and London: Verso, 2009), pg. 52

19 Alain Badiou, *The Century* (Cambridge: Polity, 2007), pg. 65-66

20 Slavoj Žižek, *The Fragile Absolute,* (Verso: New York and London, 2008), pg. 31

21 Fredric Jameson, *Marxism and Form: Twentieth-Century Dialectical Theories of Literature* (Princeton N.J. : Princeton University Press, 1974), pg. 395

22 Slavoj Žižek, *The Fragile Absolute,* (Verso: New York and London, 2008), pg. 26

23 Ibid, pg. 39

24 Ibid, pg. 31

25 Ibid, pg. 32

26 Ibid, pg. 26-27

27 Fredric Jameson, *Jameson on Jameson: conversations on cultural Marxism;* edited by Ian Buchanan. (Durham: Duke University Press, 2007), pg. 116

28 Susan Sontag, "Camp," http://interglacial.com/~sburke/pub/prose/Susan_Sontag_-_Notes_on_Camp.html

29 Yes, I'm aware I'm using a pop culture reference to explain this.

30 Susan Sontag, "Camp," http://interglacial.com/~sburke/pub/prose/Susan_Sontag_-_Notes_on_Camp.html

31 Carl Wilson, "A Spectre is Haunting Culture - The Spectre of the Hipster," April 30th, 2009, http://www.zoilus.com/documents/in-depth/2009/001688.php

32 Slavoj Žižek, *First as Tragedy Then as Farce,* (New York and London: Verso, 2009), pg. 51

33 Mark Fisher, *Capitalist Realism: Is There No Alternative?,* (Zer0

Books: Winchester, UK, 2009), pg. 5

34   Ibid, pg. 16

35   Ibid, pg. 46

36   Renata Salecl, *On Anxiety*, (London and New York: Routledge, 2004), pg. 46-47

37   Slavoj Žižek, *Plague of Fantasies*, (London and New York: Verso, 2008), pg. 24

38   Ibid, pg. 9

39   Slavoj Žižek, *How To Read Lacan*, Chapter 4, http://www.lacan.com/zizkubrick.htm

40   Fink, Bruce, *A Clinical Introduction To Lacanian Psychoanalysis: Theory And Technique*, (Cambridge, Massachusetts: Harvard University Press, 1997), pg. 186-187

41   Mark Fisher, *Capitalist Realism: Is There No Alternative?*, (Zer0 Books: Winchester, UK, 2009), pg. 56 (pg. 58 - "In conditions where realities and identities are upgraded like software, it is not surprising that memory disorders should have become the focus of cultural anxiety – see, for instance, the Bourne films, Memento, Eternal Sunshine of the Spotless Mind.")

42   Richard Sennett, *The Culture of the New Capitalism*, (New Haven: Yale University Press, 2006), pg. 3-4

43   Tiziana Terranova, "Free Labor: Producing Culture for the Digital Economy," http://www.electronicbookreview.com/thread/technocapitalism/voluntary

44   Maurizio Lazzarato, "Immaterial Labor," http://www.generation-online.org/c/fcimmateriallabour3.htm

45   Think of the difference between Windows and Linux: the former only makes money because it has copyrighted things that the latter proves that one can distribute for free

46   Claussen, Detlev, *Theodor W. Adorno: One Last Genius.* (Cambridge, Mass: Belknap Press of Harvard University Press, 2008), pg. 33

47   Austin Bunn, "Not Fade Away," *New York Times*, December 1, 2002, http://www.nytimes.com/2002/12/01/ magazine/not-

fade-away.html?pagewanted=all

48 Slavoj Žižek, *First as Tragedy Then as Farce*, (New York and London: Verso, 2009), pg. 52

49 Slavoj Žižek, *The Ticklish Subject*, (Verso: New York and London, 2008), pg. 130

50 Richard Sennett, *The Culture of the New Capitalism*, (New Haven: Yale University Press, 2006), pg. 4

51 Ibid, pg. 105

52 Ibid, pg. 4

53 Austin Bunn, "Not Fade Away," *New York Times*, December 1, 2002, http://www.nytimes.com/2002/12/01/magazine/not-fade-away.html?pagewanted=all

54 Slavoj Žižek, "A Cup of Decaf Reality," http://www.lacan.com/zizekdecaf.htm

55 Karl Marx, *Capital Vol. 1*, (New York: Modern Library: 1906), pg. 258-259

56 Slavoj Žižek, *First as Tragedy Then as Farce*, (New York and London: Verso, 2009), pg. 53

57 Ibid, pg. 147 ("It is as if the three components of the production process - intellectual planning and marketing, material production, the provision of material resources - are increasingly autonomized, emerging as separate spheres. In its social consequences, this separation appears in the guise of the 'three main classes' in today's developed societies, which are precisely not classes but three fractions of the working class: intellectual laborers, the old manual working class, and the outcasts (the unemployed, those living in slums and other interstices of public space)")

58 Slavoj Žižek, *Tarrying With The Negative*, (Durham: Duke University Press, 1993), pg. 216

59 Catherine Malabou, *What Should We Do With Our Brain?*, (New York: Fordham University Press, 2008), pg. 12

60 Slavoj Žižek, *First as Tragedy Then as Farce*, (New York and London: Verso, 2009), pg. 91